Everyday Paleo

Real Food for Real Life

FAMILY COOKBOOK

Sarah Fragoso

VICTORY BELT PUBLISHING INC.

Las Vegas

First Published in 2012 by Victory Belt Publishing Inc.

ISBN 13: 978-1-936608-63-8

Recipe Photos by Michael J. Lang, contact at michaeljlang@mac.com

Cover photo by Shannon Rosan, www.shannonrosan.com

Printed in The USA

Contents

Sauces and Dips

62 Mayonnaise

64 Everyday Paleo Ranch

66 Everyday Paleo Caesar Salad Dressing

68 Curry Spread

68 Cilantro Pesto

68 Chipotle Cream Sauce

70 Homemade Ketchup

72 Spicy Sriracha Mayo

72 Garlic Lemon Aioli

74 Brother Mark BBQ Sauce

76 Korean BBQ Sauce

78 Everyday Paleo Vinaigrette

78 Balsamic Vinaigrette

80 Cauliflower Hummus

Slow Cooker Recipes

84 Pork Green Curry

86 Family-Style Short Ribs

88 Slow Chicken Curry

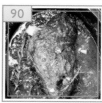
90 Slow Cooker Lamb Shank

Soups and Stews

94 Homemade Chicken Broth

96 Scrumptious Seafood Chowder

98 Tomato Soup with Chicken

100 Hungarian Stew

102 Fiesta Chicken Soup

104 Everyday Paleo Chili Verde

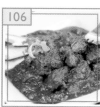
106 Everyday Paleo Chili Colorado

Meaty Meals

110 Brined and Sauced Baby Back Ribs

112 Everyday Paleo Stuffing

114 Pear and Ground Pork-Stuffed Winter Squash

116 Ground Pork and Apple Sliders

118 Best Ever Chicken Wings

120 Chicken Cacciatore

122 Whole Greek Chicken with Roasted Garlic

124 One Pot Chicken Drumsticks

Curry Chicken Salad
126

128 Chinese Chicken Salad

130 Shrimp in Horseradish Mustard Sauce

132 Coconut Shrimp Cocktail

134 Seared Ahi or Salmon

136 Tuna Patties

138 Fish Tacos with Spicy Slaw

140 Savory Salmon and Cool Peach Salsa

142 Smoked Salmon and Poached Egg Salad

144 Sloppy Joes

146 Curry Burgers

148 Spaghetti Squash and Meatballs

150 Mini Meatloaves

152 Mexican Beef Skewers

154 Vietnamese Lamb Lettuce Wraps

Egg Dishes

158 Pesto Baked Eggs

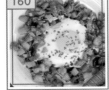
160 Winter Squash Hash and Eggs

162 Creamy Breakfast Quiche

164 Family Frittata

166 Tuna Stuffed Eggs

166 Egg Salad

Sides, Salads and Small Plates

170 Kale Chips Two Ways

172 Sweet Potato Chips

174 Turkey "Sushi" Rolls

176 Riced Cauliflower

178 Chopped Broccoli Salad

180 Roasted Beet Salad

182 Poblano Roasted Sweet Potatoes

184 Zucchini Salad

186 No Potato Salad

188 Gingered Rainbow Chard

190 Kale and Pomegranate Salad

192 Asparagus and Browned Sage "Butter"

194 Roasted Squash Bites

196 Carrot French Fries

198 Make Your Own Chopped Salad

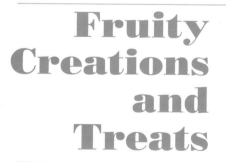
200 Zucchini Sticks

202 Simply Coleslaw

204 Kale and Parsnip Sauté

206 Spicy Slaw

Fruity Creations and Treats

210 Creamy Fruit Salad

212 Fruit Parfait

214 Pumpkin Muffins

216 Fried Banana Pudding

218 Rocket Fuel

220 Everyday Paleo Pumpkin Pie

Acknowledgments

Mom and Dad: You taught me the importance of family and how to love, and those are the two greatest gifts a parent can give to a child. Mom, even in your absence your love carries me through this journey, and when I'm feeling a little scared or doubtful, I gain strength by knowing that you would have encouraged me to go for it. And mom, I'm going for it! Thank you.

My Grandmothers: From my Grandma Ruth I learned how to be brave, kind, proud, and optimistic, and from my Grandma Katherine, I learned to be composed, loyal, and unabashed to embrace my artistic side. Thank you to my beautiful grandmothers for your lessons about love, life, and family. I miss you both deeply.

Laura, Eric, and Shaela: Thank you for your constant support and confidence. Laura, as my big sister I have looked up to you from the moment I was born, and I have always wished to be more like you. You are so incredibly special to me, and I love you with all my heart.

Mark: You are my best bud. I love hanging out with you and I will never forget the hours we spent together in the kitchen, cooking the final recipes for this book. I had so much fun being with you and being able to share this journey with you. I love you so much and I'm so lucky to be your little sis.

Coby, Jaden, and Rowan: Thank you for being my boys, for loving your mama like crazy, for putting up with me, for helping me, for encouraging me, and for believing in me. I love you so much that my heart could explode.

John: Gosh darn it, why do you have to be so great? I can't say one bad thing about you, and that's probably a good thing being that we both signed that marriage certificate and all. I can't say thank you because it's not enough. I'm sorry, but two silly words like that do not even come close to the gratitude, love, and crazy, giddy, schoolgirl-crush-like feelings that I have for you. You are the best husband a girl could possibly ask for, your fierce support and dedication to our little family is unbelievable, and our continuous, crazy adventures together are better than anything on this planet. I love you.

My friends are also my family, and I can't list everyone who's supported this project—but I'll try!

Laura H: I never knew that I believed in angels until I met you. We all love you so much and I am grateful for you everyday. Thank you so much for your help making this cookbook happen and, most importantly, thank you for loving us.

Erika S: Thank you so much for helping me with this project! You were such a hard worker, always cheerful and supportive, and I'm so glad that you were part of the cooking marathon team!

Shawn, Chrissy, Katie, and Glen: When I was a little kid I had a group of best friends, and we would wear those silly best friend bracelets, but I never really understood the true meaning of what a best friend was until I grew up and started to experience real life. Best friends are the friends who hold you up, love with you, laugh with you, cry with you, and stick around through thick and thin. It's so comforting to know that no matter what, we will always have each other. Thank you all so much for your support during this project. It has meant the world to me. Oh, and in a perfect world, I would make sure that we would always be neighbors.

Robb and Nicki: Thanks so much for your constant support. This journey never would have begun without the two of you, and for that I am eternally grateful.

Mike and America: Mike, thank you so much for taking the amazing recipe photos, and America, thank you for jumping in and helping with everything! Your love for each other and your family is infectious, and your dedication to helping others goes beyond the norm. I admire you both for your amazing spirits! Thank you for giving up so much of your time to make this book a reality.

Jason and Sheryl: Jason, not so very long ago you dropped out of the sky…ok, maybe I dropped out of the sky, but however it all happened, I'm so glad that it did! Thank you both for your love and support, and I know we'll all be friends forever. Jason, thank you for your contribution to the science in this book, and Sheryl, thank you for your recipe contributions! I couldn't have done this without the both of you.

Erich: You pretty much rock. Not sure what else to say, but thank you. I would be a little lonesome blogger with just a wish and a dream, but you decided to take a chance on *Everyday Paleo* and, well, now you are stuck with me! I'm so grateful to you and the entire Victory Belt team, and I could not be more happy or proud to be working with all of you—another awesome extension of my family.

Introduction

Welcome to the Everyday Paleo Family Cookbook!

I'm the author of the national bestselling book *Everyday Paleo* and the children's book *Paleo Pals: Jimmy and the Carrot Rocket Ship*. In my first book, *Everyday Paleo*, I relate how I found true health and wellness by adopting a healthier lifestyle, how I successfully transitioned my entire family to the Paleo diet, and how, by simply eating real food and adopting a smart exercise program, the Fragosos went from merely surviving this crazy life to thriving in it!

If you are brand new to living a Paleo lifestyle, my first book, *Everyday Paleo,* will give you a road map to get started. You will find an explanation of what eating Paleo involves, and you'll learn how to apply the principles to your life. The book you are reading now takes it a step further, offering you many recipes to nourish your body, as well as advice to help you slow down and enjoy the precious fleeting moments of your life, bringing your family closer together.

Writing my books has been wonderful for me, but the most important part of my life is my family. I am mom to three boys—Coby, Jaden, and Rowan—and wife to my best friend and husband, John. Over the last four years, we have been on an amazing journey together. We have been striving to live the healthiest life possible, and our efforts have helped us learn how to reconnect as a family.

The importance of eating right and staying connected with family were lessons that I learned as a child but had to relearn as an adult, however.

A couple of years before I started eating Paleo, I lost my beautiful, precious mother to breast cancer. Just a few weeks later, I had a chance meeting with Robb Wolf, author of *The Paleo Solution*. Thanks to Robb, I began to learn about living a Paleo lifestyle, but I did not immediately take his advice to heart.

In 2007, after the birth of my last little boy, Rowan, I found myself suffering from a long list of health complaints at the ripe old age of thirty. My ailments included chronic and painful swelling in my legs, hip bursitis, headaches, depression, fatigue, candida issues, and acne, not to mention stubborn fat that I couldn't seem to lose. Only after I became seriously ill did I finally decide to listen to my body and to the information I had received from Robb. To make a long story short, I eventually committed to trying Paleo for thirty days, and that was all the convincing I needed.

For the first time in my life, I knew what it meant to be healthy, and I never looked back. I made an incredible physical transformation, which you can see in my before and after pictures. Still, the aesthetic changes were just a bonus and a by-product of better health. I was so excited to feel good that for the first time, I began to create health-related goals that had nothing to do with the size of my jeans. My new goals were all about really living and being present in my life. Most importantly, my goals were about spending more quality time with my amazing family.

Once my Paleo journey was well on its way, I began my blog and, eventually, wrote my first book, *Everyday Paleo*, followed by my children's book, and finally this cookbook.

My degree is in psychology, and I always imagined myself as a family therapist, but I was thrown a curve ball. I was given the opportunity to intertwine my knowledge of psychology with my education in nutrition, fitness, and lifestyle, which is what you will find in this book.

I hope you enjoy the *Everyday Paleo Family Cookbook*. Please be sure to visit me at EverydayPaleo.com and our sister site, EPLifeFit.com.

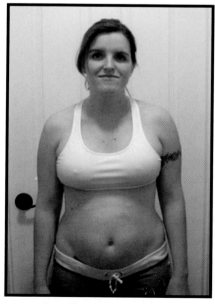

Sarah Before Picture
February 2008

Sarah After Picture
August 2008

I was raised by a mother who read to me all of the Laura Ingalls Wilder books, and not unlike the Ingalls family, we lived very simply and close to the earth. Everyone in my family loved to be in the kitchen together. It was a gathering place for food, family, and fun. I don't remember my mom "teaching" me how to cook. There was never a need to be taught because as early as I can remember, cooking together is just what we did. My mom also had no rules about what we could or couldn't eat or if we could or couldn't help. The kitchen was a safe sanctuary, warm from my mom's love and always open whenever we were hungry.

My sister, brother, and I used to come up with crazy creations in the kitchen thanks to my mom's willingness to let us experiment and her ability to give us the confidence. She knew that at some point we would need to be able to fend for ourselves, and she also knew we were capable of making our own snacks and helping with meals, even when we were very young. Of course, not all of our creations turned out to be delicious, but, as with anything else in life, we learned from our mistakes.

My brother, Mark, and I once made a cake from my mom's freshly ground whole wheat flour, only to discover that we had no frosting. I don't remember which of us came to the conclusion that mayonnaise had a similar consistency as frosting, but that's what we chose as the "perfect alternative." We mixed the creamy white stuff with cocoa powder and honey, and we slathered the cake generously with what we were sure would be delicious frosting. Well, let's just say that I can still remember exactly what that first bite tasted like. Warm mayo swirled with honey and chocolate tastes just as disgusting as it sounds. But my mom laughed with us instead of scolding us, and we learned a valuable lesson—having fun and being with family are important parts of cooking. When mistakes happen, it's better to laugh them off rather than cry over mayo-slathered cake.

Another unique aspect of my childhood was the fact that we did not watch a lot of television. Instead, we played outside, rain or shine, and I had the great privilege of learning that food comes from the earth, not from a factory. Some of my favorite memories involve planting the yearly garden with my mom, pulling weeds in the sunshine, and eating our dinner fresh picked from our own backyard. My job in the garden was to pat the soil over the seeds that my mom or dad had planted and to help keep the rows free of weeds. I learned how to distinguish between a weed and a

plant budding through the dirt, preparing to produce food for our family table. It was amazing as a kid to run outside in the morning and see that our plants had started to bud, then to taste that first cherry tomato or sugar snap pea right off the vine.

Many people considered our family to be far out and wacky because of our upbringing, but I always appreciated my mom's knowledge about nutrition and felt that nature could give us what we needed to heal what ails us. I will never take my upbringing for granted, yet I lost sight of those important lessons for a while as an adult. Eventually, I fell into a mainstream lifestyle, relying more and more on what was fast, cheap, easy, and convenient. I was overwhelmed with my less-than-natural lifestyle, and I knew that life was meant to be lived at a slower pace. But life was going too fast to change. . . or so I thought.

When my husband was in his last year of chiropractic school, Coby was only eight years old, and I was pregnant with Jaden. John and I were both commuting an hour each way from school or work. John was beginning to study for State Board exams, and I was working too many hours and feeling the repercussions of the last months of pregnancy. Add a poor diet and lack of exercise to that, and needless to say, you can be sure our lifestyle produced a constant state of exhaustion and frustration.

After one particularly long day, I opened the cupboard and became aware that all I saw were endless boxes of Hamburger Helper and Mac & Cheese. I then opened our refrigerator and saw next to nothing that resembled fresh food. I felt a rising lump in my throat, aware from my own upbringing that we could be treating our bodies a whole lot better. I was sad that my little Coby hadn't had the experiences I had as a child. His food preferences were based on boxes and supermarket aisles rather than sunshine and freshly dug dirt. I knew there had to be a better way, but I was stuck, exhausted, and not sure what to do.

While my personality always directs me to live life at full throttle, feeling awful and doing too much eventually made my entire life come to a screeching halt. Besides becoming sick from eating the wrong foods, I was sick and tired of my lifestyle, which went against my upbringing and caused a constant internal battle. I longed to relive those days with my mom in the kitchen and my simple upbringing as a child, out in the garden.

Unfortunately for me, as with many others, the beginning of great change came from great loss. When I lost my mom to breast cancer, it was the beginning of changing my lifestyle. It took a couple of years before I implemented what I had learned about Paleo, and then finally I went back to what I had always known— living close to the source of your food and even closer to the ones you love. My only wish is that we had learned about Paleo prior to my mom's cancer diagnosis.

With all of this in mind, please; ask yourself the same question that haunted me before regaining my own health: "Are we really meant to work from nine to five, come home, flip on the TV, warm up some plastic-wrapped, chemically laden meal in a box, kiss the kids good night as they stare at their video games, then get up and hit the repeat button?" I don't believe this familiar scenario is the way we're meant to live.

Before I regained my health, my entire family was slipping deeper and deeper into merely existing rather than really living. We didn't feel well and lacked the energy and drive to do more than just what was necessary, consequently missing out on simple things like playing catch or going on walks. When you live as we were at that time, these activities become challenging and are often replaced with electronic gadgets and media distractions.

Once I changed my eating habits and began to feel better, I decided to give up those old habits that our family had pretended were *real life*. It's amazing to think this life-changing decision was prompted by simply changing our nutrition. After our family started eating Paleo, I had to forfeit packaged food and plan ahead. Thanks to learning how to be prepared for even my busiest days, I had time for the activities I cherished, such as playing more with my boys. Little things like kicking the soccer ball or a rousing game of freeze tag no longer felt like a chore! Never mind that I was finally strong enough for these things—the shocking realization was that I had more family time because I had finally prioritized my time!

We gave up pizza and movie night for warm soup from the slow cooker followed by long walks, holding hands with my husband, and watching the boys run wild with delight in the setting sun. We said no to TV, and in its place found ourselves with time to *do* things, such as stacking dominos as high as skyscrapers, building forts out of couch cushions, and exploring our local hiking spot and city parks. When the rain poured outside, we stayed inside, playing board games, munching kale chips and sipping chamomile tea.

We didn't actually add hours to our day, but we subtracted the meaningless distractions so that we could enjoy moments

> *"If you focus on having fun and connecting with one another, the transition to healthier eating will be much easier."*

that will last a lifetime. Yes, it comes with hard work, dedication, and a little extra planning and preparation, but it's possible if you set your mind to it. It's all a matter of choice and finding the right tools to make life more rewarding.

Of course, with change, even positive change, there are challenges. My oldest son, Coby, struggled the most as we transitioned to a healthier lifestyle. He was twelve years old at the time we made the change. Like us, he was used to our way of life and did not like the idea of doing anything different. Coby has always been very resistant to change, and I learned early on, when he was just a toddler, that being included in the process would make it easier for him. So, instead of plowing forward and leaving Coby to lag behind, I held his hand every step of the way. We talked about why we were changing our food habits, how it would result in a healthier mom and dad and family as a whole, and how it would simply feel normal some day.

Coby was reluctant at first, but the first time I attempted a Paleo meatloaf, my usual silent-at-the-table son took a small bite, looked up at me, and said, "Wow, Mom, this is really good! I think you are figuring out this Paleo thing!" I knew that we had turned a corner!

For your family, the transition will be tuned to the personalities of everyone involved, but if you focus on having fun and connecting with one another, the transition to healthier eating will be much easier. I'm grateful to Coby for the lessons I learned during our move to Paleo. Now, he has the skills to handle change in a positive way, and seeing him grow into a confident and proud young man is a great joy to me.

Of course, I don't expect any of you to truly adopt the Laura Ingalls Wilder lifestyle and don petticoats and bonnets or move the family out to the prairie (even though it does sound tempting, minus the petticoats and bonnets). I do, however, urge you to reconsider some of your day-to-day habits and rituals in the hope that you will slow down a little bit, right along with me. Life is too short to get lost on Facebook, to be constantly late for the next commitment, and to be too tired at the end of the day to enjoy your spouse and little ones. With that in mind, embrace what you have at this moment and get back to living life a little more Everyday Paleo.

What do I mean by "living Paleo?" Does it mean just eating meat, vegetables, and healthy fat, or is there more to it than that? For me, living Paleo is about focusing on what really matters, realizing that life's pleasures have everything to do with the ones I love and very little to do with "conventional wisdom." To me, it means slowing down. Playing. Laughing. Loving. Feeling. Not missing out on the little things.

So, I invite you to join us in *really* living. We only get one shot, and as a dear friend told me not long ago, yesterday is gone, leaving us only what we have right now. I want you to embrace with me the true meaning of family, to sit around the table with your loved ones and actually listen! I want you to plop your young ones on the counter, give them a spoon, and show them what it takes to make real food! This book is meant to get you started not only on a lifelong journey of health, but also on a journey to bringing your family back to the table, strongly united, as families should be.

Along my family's Paleo journey, real food began to equal enjoying life and one another. My hope is that the advice and recipes in this book will help you find the same health and renewed joy with your family.

The Basics

First, let's look at the basics of Paleo. If this is the first time you've encountered this way of eating, you need to understand the principles of this lifestyle. I'll explain them here, but for a more comprehensive and scientific explanation, I suggest that you read The Paleo Solution *by Robb Wolf, as well as my book,* Everyday Paleo. *In the meantime, here are the basics you need to know to begin your journey.*

What Is Paleo?

The primary tenets of living a Paleo lifestyle are:

- Avoid grains, legumes, dairy, vegetable oils, refined sugar, high-fructose corn syrup, artificial sweeteners, and all other highly processed foods.

- Eat meat from animals that lived the way nature intended their species to live—e.g., cattle fed on grass.

- Eat both vegetables and fruit, but eat more vegetables than fruits.

- Eat quality fats like avocado and coconut oil. Eat nuts and seeds, but in moderation.

Why the above set of rules? These are the dietary guidelines that nature intended for us to follow. The Paleo diet is the human diet without intervention, and eating this way emphasizes the importance of living as close as possible to the way human beings lived before agriculture and before the growing and processing of grains. Eating Paleo means getting back to the basics of food, the foods we ate when we had to hunt and gather in order to survive, rather than rely on modern-day conveniences and highly processed food sources.

Of course, actually hunting and gathering your food is usually not possible for modern-day people like us, but living a Paleo lifestyle is still entirely possible. If this is the first you've heard of this way of eating, your mind is probably racing with questions about how something that seems so contrary to mainstream nutrition advice can possibly be right. I will briefly explain why Paleo makes sense from a simple scientific standpoint, but, again, I urge you to continue with your own research and read, read, read to learn more.

But We NEED Grains, Right? Grains Are Good for You, Aren't They?

On the contrary, grains are good for birds, not people. Grains contain gut-irritating lectins that damage the microvilli, or brush border, in our intestines, which then leads to the widening of tight junctions, a condition also known as leaky gut. This condition allows larger particles than are meant to go through the digestive system to pass through the gut wall and into your body. Some of these particles, especially the lectins themselves and gram-negative bacteria, can be very problematic. When your immune system discovers these interlopers, it destroys them and creates an antibody to go hunting for more. Unfortunately, the interlopers can sometimes resemble various tissues in your body, which can confuse your immune system, causing it to attack your own cells. When this happens, you become "autoimmune." Autoimmune diseases are situations in which your immune system has waged war against one or more of your own tissues. Rheumatoid arthritis, cataracts, ankylosing spondylitis, Hashimoto's disease, eczema, and Celiac disease are just a few examples of autoimmune diseases plaguing Western society. Fortunately, several of them respond very well to the removal of the offending agents from your diet.

This is not the only reason to avoid grains, however. All of that gut damage elevates systemic inflammation, which makes your immune system work overtime. Obviously, that isn't a good thing. Chronic inflammation can lead to noninfectious diseases and is a serious situation that should not be taken lightly. I could write an entire book on this, but I'm not a scientist. Suffice it to say that science has blamed many of today's most common life-threatening diseases on chronic inflammation. Read Robb Wolf's book, or look it up. If this is new information for you, it will be very eye opening.

But We NEED Dairy, Right?

Cow's milk is intended for baby cows. Unfortunately, cow's milk can be problematic for children and adults alike. For instance, milk elevates serum levels of something called Insulin-Like Growth Factors (IGF), which increase the risk of *all* cancers. Cow's milk also raises insulin levels and contributes to insulin resistance, a condition that increases your risk of heart disease, stroke, type-2 diabetes, obesity, and Alzheimer's disease. Cow's milk overall is better off avoided by everyone; it is not necessary or essential to the growth and development of children and offers no real health benefits for adults.

What about the other forms of dairy like hard cheese, cottage cheese, butter, and sour cream? Butter and heavy cream are relatively benign because most everything but the fat has been removed from them, but they can still be problematic if they come from grain-fed cows or if you have an autoimmune issue. My advice is to avoid all dairy products, butter, and heavy cream included, for the first thirty days that you try Paleo. Then, experiment with butter and heavy cream to assess how you feel.

Is Vegetable Oil Okay?

Vegetable and seed oils, like corn oil, for example, are predominantly linoleic acid, which is an omega-6 fatty acid that easily turns rancid. If you have too much omega-6 in your diet, you develop chronic, systemic inflammation. As you can imagine, our culture's mass consumption of vegetable oils is a primary factor in our increased incidence of diseases such as heart disease, cancer, and osteoporosis, just to name a few. It is best to avoid vegetable oil and to stick to healthy oils such as coconut oil, olive oil, and other healthy fat sources, which can be found on page 21.

Eat Meat! But What About All That Saturated Fat?

The "artery-clogging saturated fat" myth, or lipid hypothesis, may finally be approaching the end of its life due to all the good science that has surfaced in the last decade, but it is unfortunately not going down without a fight. The lipid hypothesis states that saturated fat increases cholesterol levels, and cholesterol, in turn, causes heart disease. For a fantastic commentary on the political aspects of how we became so enchanted with such fiction, watch the movie *Fat Head*, by Tom Naughton.

The truth is that there has never been any substantial evidence that the consumption of saturated animal fat from pasture-raised animals correlates to high cholesterol, heart disease, or any other disease for that matter.

The real villains of heart disease appear to be chronic inflammation and things called glycation and triglycerides. For more detailed information on this subject and the biochemistry involved, read the already mentioned *The Paleo Solution* by Robb Wolf.

Why Does Grass-Fed Matter?

Contrary to the diet of most beef cattle today, the natural diet of cattle is simply grass. Unfortunately, the big food companies do not agree. Instead, most of our cows are fed corn because it puts a lot of weight on the animals in a shorter period of time and gives them more intramuscular fat or marbling. According to the enlightening documentary, *Food Inc*, about 70 percent of the corn grown in the United States is fed to cattle. That's a lot of corn being eaten by animals that do not eat corn when left alone to their own devices. The problem is that cows, just like humans, pay a price for intervention. Corn-feeding changes the polyunsaturated fatty acid (PUFA) profile in beef, increasing the omega-6: omega-3 ratio in the fat. When we eat this beef, the resulting increased omega-6: omega-3 ratio in our bodies causes more of that nasty chronic inflammation. Remember, too much inflammation in the body correlates with the majority of all modern-day diseases.

With that fact in mind, the prescription is simple: Eat cows that eat grass. It's not nearly as challenging as some think to find grass-fed meat, and I have included sources in the reference section of this book to help you find quality meat in your area. Cost per pound varies a great deal depending on the supplier. I suggest investigating sources in your area to find a supplier within your price range. You can often cut down the cost by buying a whole animal and storing the meat in the freezer. If you simply can't get grass-fed meat, do not throw in the towel and give up entirely on eating Paleo. Eating conventionally-farmed meat is still better than eating highly processed grain-based foods, so don't go back to your bagels. Just eat leaner cuts of meat and supplement with omega 3 fish oils.

Basic Food Guide:

Meat (Protein)

Chicken

Turkey

Duck

Beef

Pork

Lamb

Veal

Bison

Venison

Elk

Eggs

Jerky (StevesOriginal.com or PaleoBrands.com)

Organ meats

Fish & Seafood (Protein)

Salmon

Tilapia

Crab

Shrimp

Tuna

Cod

Vegetables (Carbohydrates)

Artichoke

Asparagus

Beets

Broccoli

Brussels sprouts

Cabbage

Carrots

Cauliflower

Celery

Collards/mustard

Greens/kale

Cucumber

Eggplant

Endive

Lettuce, spinach

Mushrooms

Onions

Parsley

Parsnip

Peppers

Radish

Seaweed

Squash (all types)

Sweet potatoes/yams

Fruit
(Carbohydrates)

Tomato

Lemons/limes

Apple

Apricot

All berries

All melons

Fig

Grapefruit

Kiwi

Nectarine

Orange

Peach

Pear

Plum

Pomegranate

Tangerine

Watermelon

In Moderation

Dried fruit (no sugar added)

Tropical fruits such as:

- Banana
- Mango
- Pineapple
- Guava

Fats

Avocado

Olive oil

Coconut oil

Coconut milk

Coconut flakes (unsweetened)

Almonds

Brazil nuts

Chestnuts

Hazelnuts

Macadamia nuts

Pecans

Pine nuts

Pistachios

Walnuts

Pumpkin seeds

Sesame seeds

Almond butter

Organic grass-fed heavy cream (unless you have an autoimmunity issue)

Organic grass-fed ghee

Organic grass-fed butter (unless you have an autoimmunity issue)

Lard, tallow

Spices

Allspice

Anise

Basil

Bay leaf

Caraway

Cardamom

Cayenne powder

Chili powder

Cilantro

Cinnamon

Cloves

Coriander

Cumin

Curry powder

Dill

Fenugreek

Garlic

Ginger

Marjoram

Mint

Mustard

Nutmeg

Oregano

Paprika

Parsley

Pepper

Rosemary

Saffron

Sage

Tarragon

Thyme

Turmeric

Vanilla

Getting Started

Family Matters

What happened to the good ol' days? Back before the Kardashians, SpongeBob, *Halo*, *Call of Duty*, *Survivor*, and yes, *The Bachelor* (gasp!), how did we survive? I'm not talking about back in the 1940s or even the 1920s. I'm talking about before we had the majority of today's modern conveniences, when what really mattered was taking care of the family. I'm not suggesting that today's society cares less about day-to-day care or bonding with their children and loved ones. What I'm suggesting is that we have taken on too much and have become overwhelmed with the enormous amount of input constantly coming at us from all directions. We are bombarded with more choices than we know how to handle, and we're expected to "do it all." The problem is that this takes away from what we are "doing it all" for—time to spend with the ones we love.

I believe it takes conscious effort to decide how much you will allow today's modern society to take you over. You must admit that in order to find balance, you have to make some serious choices about where and how you focus your attention. I am in the same boat as the rest of you, and it's a daily struggle to not continually flip open the laptop just to "check in." I have to fight the impulse to put in a status update on my trusty iPhone every few minutes or calculate or tweet or e-mail or text or weather-check or Amazon-search. I remind myself that countless hours of time well spent nurturing myself and my family can be lost in the blink of an eye thanks to modern technology.

Don't get me wrong; I'm grateful for today's modern conveniences, but I have to be diligent to constantly balance all that is available and accessible in order to enjoy what's happening in the moment. Each moment is precious, and only with great loss do we usually realize just how fleeting they are.

The youngest among us are often the greatest teachers. When my Rowan was about three, he tried to get my attention while I was texting on my phone. I sat down next to him and pretended to listen as I continued texting. Rowan crawled into my lap, placed his hands on either side of my face, lifted my head up to look into his eyes, and calmly said, "Mom, you can't listen to me with your phone." Oh, so true! From that moment on, I implemented my "no phones when kids need to tell me something rule," and I know I'm not missing anything from my phone. Instead, I have gained precious time thanks to choosing to *disconnect* from staying constantly "*connected.*"

With that thought in mind, let's explore some ideas as to how you can make room for more play, laughter, and love, and how you can successfully include your family in your Paleo journey. I'll explain what children *really* need in order to grow up mentally and physically healthy (and it isn't nonfat milk or fortified cereals). I'll also offer time-saving tips and tricks that will help lessen the hours you spend in the kitchen, along with a week-long meal plan, shopping list, school lunch ideas, and a budget guide. Finally, you will find strategies to optimally plan and prepare meals in order to spend abundant time with the people you love.

> *"Each moment is precious and fleeting and often only with great loss do we realize how fleeting these moments are."*

Getting Back to the Cave

I'm not asking you to show up barefoot to work with a spear in hand, ready to kill the pigeons and squirrels across the street in the park for your lunch. Nor am I asking you to forgo showering and shaving or suggesting you move to the mountains and find an actual cave to live in (although that would be kind of cool). What I'm asking you to figure out is how you can reprioritize your life a little and slow down enough to discover that health and wellness are not only about nutrition and exercise. Your well-being is also about surrounding yourself with people you love and about living fully in the moment. I don't mean taking enough videos and pictures to store on your laptop to feel as if you experienced those moments, I'm talking about truly being *present*.

This concept of slowing down may seem silly to some people, but as I work on this in my own life, I notice that I feel more alive and less stressed when I'm diligent about following these ideas. I'm also less guilt-ridden about not paying enough attention to the ones I love, and most importantly, my kids are happier, too. The following ideas will give you a lot to think about, so don't feel overwhelmed. Please feel free to tweak these suggestions to make them work for your family.

1.
It feels good to be heard.

Turn off the phone or the computer or the TV or any other electronic device that might distract you while your little ones tell you something important. This is tough because what kids tell you may *always* be important, and you can't *always* stop everything to listen intently. But you do know when it really matters, so take the time to crouch down to their height level, ignore everything else, and soak up every precious word in order to respond accordingly. Kids love it when they are really heard, and believe it or not, by simply listening intently to your children, you will see a decrease in behavioral issues. Why? Because they will stop fighting to gain your validation. We have to remember that to a child, what they are upset or excited about feels just as important to them as what we adults might feel upset or excited about; even if what they are telling us might seem trivial. It feels so good to be heard! As adults, we understand this; *we* want to be heard when we have something important to say, and so do children. This one small act will give you minutes in your day with your kids that you didn't realize you had. That phone call or text can wait. When your kids need to talk to you, they shouldn't be put on hold.

Ask real questions, and request real responses as you gather around the dinner table. But, first and foremost, make it a rule that you all eat dinner *together and at the table*. The following questions are *not* allowed: "What did you learn at school today?" "How was work, honey?" Those questions are boring and meaningless. I want you to get your family really talking! Here's one way to do it: When you sit down together, ask each child, "What was the best thing that happened to you today, and what was the worst thing that happened to you today?" Grownups, you get a turn, too. Our kids love this conversation starter. They get to fill the family in on events that they might have forgotten about otherwise, and we all get caught up in the moments of their day that mattered most. Also, our kids have a chance to hear us talk about our days as well, and that makes them feel included and important. I often get amazing advice from my own children that surprises and delights me! My kids sometimes report that there was nothing "worse," that it all was good. But if there was a worst moment, this is our chance as a family to work through it. Usually, we all come out the other side of it laughing.

Play just for the fun of it! I was only eighteen years old when Coby was born, and I was very distracted when playing with my little guy because, well, most eighteen-year-olds are easily distracted. I was young and naive, but fortunately, my own amazing mom taught me a very important lesson early in Coby's life: Your little ones are little only once; soon they will be grown, and you'll wish for those days of hot wheel tournaments and dress-up parties. She was so right, and I'm glad I listened. I have found that if I let go of everything else on my mind when I'm playing with my children, I really do have fun. Kids learn through play. They learn how to interact properly, how to be social, and how to make positive choices. Children actually work through their problems by playing. Unlike adults, they are not capable of always talking about their feelings, but they can play and act out their frustrations safely with you. So remember, playing with your children is not for the sole purpose of entertaining them. When playing sounds difficult, I think about what I would be missing out on if I didn't get down to the height level of my children, and what my children would miss out on sharing with me. I would miss the leaves shaped like elephants and the clouds dancing, and the ant that is strong enough to carry a load twice as big as his body. All of these little wonders pointed out to me by my children are so

2.
Ask real questions and request real responses as you gather around the dinner table.

3.
Playing for the fun of it.

much more interesting than my Facebook status updates, and noticing the difference in the way my children behave when we take the time to really play is all the proof and encouragement I need. For more information on the importance of play, I suggest the book, *The Power of Play*, by David Elkind and *Play: How It Shapes the Brain, Opens the Imagination, and Invigorates the Soul*, by Stuart Brown, MD.

4.
Spend more time in nature with your family.

Spend more time in nature with your family. After you read this sentence, whether it's dark or light, go outside and look up at the sky. Ponder only that very moment. Take deep breaths of air, relax, and really look at what you see. Do this as a family. It seems hippy-dippy, I know, but you know what this little exercise is? It's called really living. Not to mention the scientific proof that simply being outside improves mood and relieves stress, and when you're out during the daylight, you soak up the benefits of much-needed vitamin D from the sun. If your kids aren't excited about being outside, there are simple ways to change that. Buy or make a bird feeder, and find a place to hang it. Then, get ready for some bird-watching fun! Look for bugs with your kids. Little ones love things like spider webs, crawling ants, pollinating bees on flowers, and garden snails. Help them notice these things, and they'll beg to go outside again the next day! Plant a garden, and if you don't have room or a backyard, plant herbs or flowers in small flowerpots to put on your porch or the window sill. Make it a family affair to find all of the parks or places to hike in your area, and turn it into an adventure over the summer months to visit and explore each one. Create a journal together of your park adventures. Really living is not complicated; it's the smallest things that matter and the little details that you will remember later in your life. That's what I want for my family, and that's what I want for yours, too.

5.
Schedule your technology time.

Schedule your technology time. Make a written agreement with yourself about the time you will spend on your computer and the time you will allow yourself to enjoy social media. The computer is a time warp. There is an entire world at your fingertips, and it's exciting and fun and incredibly useful. Unfortunately, you can get caught up and sucked in so deeply that you might forget about the world that you're actually living in. My career sprouted on the Web, so trust me, I love it, but like you, I have to find balance. You might go through withdrawal when you make this change, but it's worth it. Here's a suggested schedule: Spend only fifteen minutes in the morning checking in, visiting your favorite sites (like EverydayPaleo.com), and printing out anything you might need for the day, such as recipes or shopping lists. Give yourself thirty minutes in the afternoon when the kids are doing homework or are otherwise occupied. Most important, give yourself *at least* two full days a week in which you take a total break from anything technology related. I understand that because of work this break might not be possible, but if you have to check in because your career depends on it, *do only work-related activities* on your technology-free days and stay away from any surfing, tweeting, shopping, or updating. Technology-free days are good for weekends when families spend the most time together.

Schedule your children's technology time. Remember, *you* are the parent, you are in charge, and if you make the rules and stick to them, your kids will respect and love you for it (although they might not act that way at first). I know that TV and video games are easy to turn to because they keep the kids occupied so that you can "get stuff done," but why aren't the kids helping you get that "stuff" done? We need to focus on bringing up a responsible generation, one that understands there is work to be done in order to survive, and, believe it or not, kids *like* to have responsibility. I'll talk more later about the specific emotional needs of children, but for now, I just want to suggest that you start scheduling your kids' electronic time. You'll be amazed at the creativity, better moods, and decreased misbehavior that will result from limiting their time in front of games, computers, and television.

Here is a suggested technology schedule: thirty minutes of computer games twice a week, one hour of video games on the weekend, thirty minutes of television in the evening (or, better yet, *no* television during the week). Of course, play with this schedule to make it work for your family, but this is a good starting point. Want to hear something crazy? I suggest you get rid of your cable service all together. Beyond adding to quality time spent with one another, no cable TV will save you money! Trashing the TV was such a freeing feeling. I'm not telling you to follow suit; I'm simply sharing my own experience. Nixing the cable TV has brought us all closer together. In the evening, when the kids

6.
Schedule your children's technology time.

are in bed, I actually talk to my husband, get caught up on Everyday Paleo stuff, and go to bed at a decent hour. Think about it—trashing your tube might be the best thing you ever do.

7.
Just Say No.

Just Say No! Do you find yourself constantly rushing to the next thing without really enjoying what's happening then and there? Are you always pushing your kids out the door, cramming them quickly into their car seats, snapping at them to hurry up, and wondering why you have so few hours in the day? Maybe you need to cut back a little! Do you *have* to have your kids in karate, banjo, ballet, archery, and gymnastics, or do you think that maybe just one or two of those activities will still result in fabulous and well-rounded children? Do you say yes to every volunteer day, race day, pledge event, sponsorship, or request for a chaperone, party coordinator, or teacher's aide? Yet, have you forgotten the last time you sat down with your kids and played a game of cards?

What kids really need from their parents is simple: They need you to be present in their lives, and they need plenty of time to play. They don't need to be enriched by every enrichment program in existence. They need to be loved, and they need you to listen to them. They need rules, boundaries, and responsibilities. They need freedom to express themselves. They need to feel as though they are a contributing part of their family unit so that they grow up understanding what it means to take care of themselves and others. This will help them to raise their own children to become contributing members of society. They need you to slow down, and they need to cook dinner with you, sit down and talk, and play. That's it. They just need *you*. So, the next time someone asks you to head the PTA and plan the next 300 field trips and correct the spelling papers all before Tuesday, just say no!

8.
Have a date night.

Have a date night. What does this have to do with bringing the family closer together? Everything! If you feel overworked, stressed out, and disconnected from your significant other, you should probably reconnect. And no better way than to steal a few minutes or even a few hours alone.

Now, here's a wild idea: Beyond the occasional weekend night out, try to have date night once a week in the middle of the week, even when the kids have homework. Sound like a bad idea? No way, and here's how you do it: Put your kids in charge of creating a special evening for their parents! If your kids are too young to cook on their own, prepare something earlier in the day,

and make a plan. Have your little ones set the table with pretty flowers and candles. Put all the food in easy-to-carry bowls, and let your kids serve you. Allow them to then eat their dinner in another room on blankets like a picnic, or let this be their movie night while you two have dinner together *alone*.

If your kids are older, they can cook for you and serve you! Kids really get into this, pretending to be your server, refilling your water glass, bringing you more food at your request. This is such a great way to model love and connection to your kids and the importance of spending quality time with your spouse. Of course, this will not be as quiet and serene as a night *out* alone, but it's a ton of fun and a great way to let the kids feel like they have done something amazing for you!

Take turns planning meals. There are so many Paleo cookbooks out there now, plus websites galore with millions of meal options, that not knowing what to make for dinner is no longer a problem. Even so, folks sometimes get stuck in the same routine. There's nothing wrong with that if it works for your family, but it's still nice to mix it up a bit. This is where taking turns planning meals can keep your food life exciting. Alternate weeks in which each of you decides what's on the menu. Help your kids do the planning by explaining to them which meals are good for leftovers and what nights you need to have a slow cooker meal option or which days you have a little more flexibility to make something more complicated or time-consuming. This is a great way to teach children about budgeting, shopping, and which vegetables are in season. Finally, take a trip together to the farmers market to find out what's available, and let the meal planning fun begin!

Have a "plate to share." This is a fun idea given to me by Beverly Meyer of *Primal Diet, Modern Health* and a wonderful way to introduce new foods to the family without making a big deal out of it. At mealtime, place a large tray or several small plates in the middle of the table with small piles of different food items. Some suggestions include olives, cubed or sliced veggies such as jicama and bell pepper slices, possibly some artichoke hearts, or leftover pieces of steak or chicken, small pieces of cauliflower or broccoli, celery sticks, or anything else in bite-sized pieces. Consider including guacamole or some of the other dip options in the recipe section of this book, like my Paleo Ranch. This is a wonderful way to introduce new foods to your children without making it obvious.

9.
Take turns planning meals.

10.
Have a "plate to share."

The Reality of Television (Not Reality Television)

I already mentioned what a time-waste television can be, but I also want to share a few statistics gathered by the A.C. Nielsen Co. found at http://www.csun.edu/science/health/docs/tv&health.html about television viewing and the family. If everyone in the developed world read the stats here, we would probably hear a collective "thud" as families tossed their TVs in the nearest dumpster. (Well, it's better to recycle them, but it's still a fun thought!)

Here are the actual stats on how plugged in we really are:

99%
Percentage of households that possess at least one television

66%
Percentage of U.S. homes with three or more TV sets

66%
Percentage of Americans who regularly watch television while eating dinner

$1.25 trillion
Value of that time assuming an average wage of $5/hour

6 million
Number of videos rented daily in the U.S.

49%
Percentage of Americans who say they watch too much TV

2.24
Number of TV sets in the average U.S. household

6 hours, 47 min.
Number of hours per day that TV is on in an average U.S. home

250 billion
Number of hours of TV watched annually by Americans

56%
Percentage of Americans who pay for cable TV

3 million
Number of public library items checked out daily

The average American watches more than four hours of TV each day, or twenty-eight hours per week. That's two months of nonstop TV-watching per year. In a sixty-five-year life, that person will have spent nine years just watching television.

4000
Approximate number of studies examining TV's effects on children

3.5
Number of minutes per week that parents spend in meaningful conversation with their children

Children and Television

1680
Number of minutes per week that the average child watches television

70%
Percentage of daycare centers that use TV during a typical day

73%
Percentage of parents who would like to limit their children's TV watching

54%
Percentage of 4–6-year-olds who, when asked to choose between watching TV and spending time with their father, preferred television

900
Hours per year the average American youth spends in school

1500
Hours per year the average American youth watches television

20000
Number of 30-second TV commercials seen in a year by the average child

2 million
Number of TV commercials seen by the average person by age 65

Commercialism

92%
Percentage of survey participants (1993) who said that TV commercials aimed at children make them too materialistic

1
Rank of food products/fast food restaurants among TV advertisements to kids

$15 billion
Total spending by 100 leading TV advertisers in 1993

30%
Percentage of local TV news broadcast time devoted to advertising

53.8%
Percentage devoted to stories about crime, disaster, and war

General

Other

0.7%
Percentage devoted to public service announcements

Understanding Kids

In *Everyday Paleo,* I wrote about the ways to get started on this Paleo journey and how to engage the family in this lifestyle. One of my first suggestions is to get rid of all the food in your house that you *and* your children should not be eating, making way for *only* Paleo food items. This is the only sure way to stick to eating as healthy as possible, especially within that first month of transitioning to Paleo. If you keep "special treats" in the house, you and the kids will cave in to the temptation. Your kids will beg, whine, and nag you for the ice cream or cookies that you still have around, and you will inevitably give in. Then, the vicious cycle will continue.

Kids want to feel healthy, too, but unless you give them the chance, they won't experience what it feels like to eat real, wholesome food.

With my own family, we made the transition cold turkey. I tossed the non-Paleo foods overnight, and we started the very next day. This plan worked out well for us, but it might not be the approach you want to use with your own children. Every family is different, as is every child, and a gradual approach might be best, depending on your situation. Remember my experience with Coby—he managed the change just fine with extra care and attention. My two youngest children hardly took any notice (granted Rowan was an infant at the time and knew no different and Jaden has always been my kid that would eat anything put in front of him.)

Using the following information, you can determine the best way to get your family on board. It could be extremely challenging to get kids who are totally carb dependent off the pasta or crackers immediately, so make the transition one meal at a time. Start with breakfast for a week or so, move on to lunch, and then to dinner, slowly ridding your house of the junk. Refer back to what you are about to read below, and stay consistent! Be open, honest, and cheerful, and remember that you are the parent and you're making the best decisions possible for the health of your family.

As parents, we want our children to be happy. We like to give them what they want, and, of course, we provide them with what they need to be safe, warm, loved, and cared for. We also set rules, create boundaries, and teach them how to make the best decisions they can through life. For some reason, though, many parents find it difficult to get rid of the food they believe makes their children happy. Taking away the junk food is not cruel. It's one of the kindest, most loving acts you can do as a parent. Feeding your children real food cannot be classified as a traumatic experience!

If you approach this change with a positive outlook, joy, and happiness, your children are sure to follow suit. If you grumble and gripe about no longer having cereal for breakfast, your little ones will, too. If you hand them a spatula and show them how to crack eggs as you laugh and giggle together, no one will *miss* the cereal. To further prove my point that kids *can* be happy without the "kid food" that our media so diligently pours down our throats, let's look at the basic needs of children and you will be able to determine for yourself if tossing out the mac and cheese, toaster pastry strudels, and Cheerios will actually tarnish them for life.

The basic needs of a child

- Food, water, and shelter

- Love, security, stability

- Parental attention

- Individuality and self-expression

- Self-efficacy (belief in their own competence) and responsibility

- Recognition

- Stimulation and new experiences

- Boundaries

- Routine

Nowhere on this list do you see fish-shaped crackers. Provide a new routine of healthier food choices, and do not go back and forth, letting unhealthy food in and out of your home. That's simply confusing for the entire family. Dedicate yourself to living a healthier Paleo lifestyle, and stick to it. This does not mean that you can never again have treats, but you can make healthier choices. Trust me, I have yet to meet anyone who doesn't enjoy whipped coconut cream atop mountains of fresh berries or the occasional blueberry pancakes made with almond meal and mashed bananas.

Children thrive on new experiences and stimulation!

Take them with you to a farm, and show them where organic vegetables grow. One of the best experiences we've had as a family was joining a local farm-share cooperative. Once a week, I take my kids to the farm where our vegetables are grown. They chat with the farmers, see where our food comes from, observe the hard work involved in producing the food, and help me fill our basket with that week's bounty. We often get to wander into the fields and pick cherry tomatoes or see new plants budding. My children can ask all the questions they like, watch the chickens pecking at the large compost pile, and fill their hands with fresh eggs for the week. They get dirty, soak up sunshine, and munch on carrots during the car ride home. If a farm share is not possible for your family, that's all right. Instead, take them to an outdoor farmers market or even a health food store to discover new vegetables and fruits together. Let them pick out new items to try. Learn together about sustainable agriculture, plant herbs in a planter box in your home, or start a garden in your own backyard. Cook together, discuss what new foods you like best, and relax, because it's okay if asparagus is yucky and sweet potatoes are awesome.

Praise your kids for the help they give you but not the food they eat. Stop watching your kids like a hawk at the dinner table, and do not have a running commentary over every bite they take. In fact, when you sit down for dinner, pay *no* attention to what does or does not go into their mouths. If you make it a big deal, *they'll* make it a big deal. Put food on the table, talk about your day, laugh, have fun, and eat. If your child grumbles or is upset with the food options, simply say, "Well, that's what we're having today," and stop at that one simple sentence. Nothing more needs to be said. They will eat, I promise. Your kids may not show excitement about the new food overnight, but it will happen. The more attention you pay to other areas of your child's life and the less attention you give to his or her food preferences, the more relaxed your child will become about trying new tastes.

In our home, I never even ask my kids if they like what they're eating. If I give them the option to not like it, they probably won't, so leaving out that question has been paramount in successfully getting my children to try new things. If your kids find a new favorite or really hate something, trust me, they'll let you know without you needing to ask! If you stick to this plan, you'll soon realize that your kids don't wake up in the morning wondering if you're going to feed them. They wake up wondering what new and exciting moments their day will bring, so try to make this journey new and exciting. Focus on the positive, give your children responsibilities, and offer them new experiences. The journey promises to be a rewarding and life-changing one for your family, but remember that it will be what you make it.

The Lunch Box for Kids and Grownups Too

Preparing a Paleo lunch can be the most challenging part of making the transition to this lifestyle, simply because it's difficult to figure out what to use for packing the food. Fortunately, there are now several wonderful lunch boxes or other types of containers available. I personally learned the hard way and found myself frustrated and overwhelmed. At first, Jaden appeared after school with food dripping out of his lunch box and unsealed plastic bags. He was always cheerful about eating Paleo, but the lunch box messes were embarrassing. Finally, after a bit of research, I realized that what I needed was the right container. Then, packing Paleo lunches became just as easy as packing our old lunches in the past.

Furthermore, the longer we eat Paleo, the more aware my kids become. When Jaden was in first grade, he came home from school one day and reported with concern what his classmate had brought for lunch. His friend had a hot dog, Hot Cheetos, M&M's, and a Capri sun. Jaden said his friend told him that his tummy hurt after eating the M&Ms, but they tasted so good that he ate them anyway. My Jaden looked up at me and said, "Mom, I'm so glad that my lunch doesn't make my tummy hurt!" A statement like that is worth the extra bit of effort it takes to plan lunches for the week, and my hope is that other families continue to learn the benefits of following a more natural way of eating so that no one eats a lunch that makes his or her tummy ache!

Here are the lunch containers that we use, which I highly recommend:

- Planet Box stainless steel lunch boxes found at PlanetBox.com. (Our Planet Box has lasted almost three years, and the only thing we have had to replace is the carrying case. The lunch box itself appears to be indestructible and has more than paid for itself by now.)

- Lunch Bots food containers and insulated containers found at LunchBots.com. (I love the smaller Lunch Bot for snacks and always have one packed and ready to go for long car rides or outings to the park.)

EVERYDAY PALEO FAMILY COOKBOOK

- Klean Kanteen Insulated Thermos found at KleanKanteen. com. (I live in Chico, California, and this local company is doing great work to keep our environment healthy and clean. The Klean Kanteen insulated containers are wonderful for keeping hot soups, stews, and meatballs warm for hours.)

As far as what to put in those lunch boxes, I'll give you several sample school lunches, many of which are derived from recipes found in this book.

- **Lunch 1**: Mini Meatloaves (p. 150), carrot sticks with Paleo Ranch (p. 64), strawberries and blueberries

- **Lunch 2**: Brined and Sauced Baby Back Ribs (p. 110), apple slices and almond butter

- **Lunch 3**: Applegate Farms turkey slices wrapped around avocado slices, black olives, cucumber slices, and celery with almond butter and raisins

- **Lunch 4**: Curry Burger (p. 146), coconut flakes, and dried apples

Lunch Box "Menus"

- **Lunch 5**: Chinese Chicken Salad (p. 128)

- **Lunch 6**: Ground Pork and Apple Slider (p. 116) with Homemade Ketchup (p. 70), Sweet Potato Chips (p. 172), sliced kiwi

- **Lunch 7**: Egg Salad (p. 166) with cucumber slices for scooping, black olives, mandarin orange sections

- **Lunch 8**: Turkey Sushi Rolls (p. 174), grapes, coconut flakes

- **Lunch 9**: Spaghetti Squash and Meatballs (p. 148)

- **Lunch 10**: Ham slices, Cauliflower Hummus (p. 80) with carrot, celery, or jicama sticks, and strawberries

- **Lunch 11**: Tuna-Stuffed Eggs (p. 166), and an orange

- **Lunch 12**: Tomato Soup with Chicken (p. 98), carrots and broccoli with Paleo Ranch (p. 64), banana sliced in half and spread with almond butter

- **Lunch 13**: Applegate Farms salami slices, hard-boiled egg, Kale Chips (p. 170), Rocket Fuel (p. 218)

- **Lunch 14**: Leftover sliced Roasted Greek Chicken (p. 122), cucumber slices, Creamy Fruit Salad (p. 210)

- **Lunch 15**: Family Frittata (p. 164), melon chunks

Quick and Simple Meal Ideas

Quite a few of the recipes in this book are quick and simple meals, and the preparation and cooking times of all recipes are marked. Quick and easy meals for the family are a must-have, and the ones that follow are fast and minimalistic ideas for hectic days. (No matter how much you try to slow down, you'll still have a few hectic days!) Be sure, however, to take a couple of hours on the weekend to prepare for the week ahead.

Here are some simple prep suggestions to make your wildest days feel much less crazy:

1. Make some Mayonnaise (p. 62)! Having mayo ready to go will help with meal prep and give you a base for several sauce or dip suggestions in this book. Also, make half of your mayo into Paleo Ranch (p. 64).

2. Make Homemade Ketchup (p. 70).

3. Make Brother Mark BBQ Sauce (p. 74).

4. Make the homemade salad dressing recipes (p. 66 and p. 78).

5. Make Cilantro Pesto (p. 68).

6. Make Homemade Chicken Broth and beef broth (p. 94). This is a great staple to have on hand for quick additions to several recipes in this book.

7. Make some Cauliflower Hummus (p. 80). Quick snacks and fast additions to lunches are a must, and this dip is delicious and convenient to have on hand.

8. Dice some onions! Take 2–3 onions, dice them up, and seal them in an airtight container. They'll be good for at least 3–4 days. I also recommend keeping diced onions in the freezer so that you can break off a chunk when you need

them. Diced onions keep well in the freezer for up to a month.

9.   Mince some garlic, or purchase already minced or crushed garlic.

10.   Defrost some meat. There's nothing worse than coming home to a huge freezer full of frozen food. Plan your week, and defrost what you'll need.

11.   Hard-boil some eggs. I always have at least a dozen hard-boiled eggs on hand for quick breakfasts or snacks, Egg Salad (p. 166), or as an addition to tuna or chicken salad.

12.   Brown some ground beef. If you already have a couple of pounds of ground beef cooked and ready, some of the recipes that follow will be ready to eat that much faster.

13.   Sprinkle some chicken thighs and breasts with sea salt and black pepper, and pan-fry them in coconut oil. They cook quickly and taste yummy, and you can have a meal in minutes on those crazy weeknights or when you need to quickly pack your lunch before you head out the door to work. I slice up the chicken breasts to add to lunch boxes or top salads.

14.   Slice some veggies. Some folks worry about nutrient loss when storing sliced veggies, so to keep them as nutrient-rich and fresh as possible, simply store them in an airtight container. I like to have sliced cucumbers, carrots, celery, bell peppers, and jicama on hand for fast snacking and quick lunch box additions. Remember the Cauliflower Hummus I suggested you have on hand as well? It's perfect for dipping the veggies, and the combo makes for a quick snack that's ready to go when you need it.

15.   Properly store your fresh herbs. There's nothing like having fresh herbs to liven up your meals, but keeping them fresh for longer than a day or two can be challenging. To help your fresh herbs last a bit longer, snip off the ends of the stems of your cilantro, basil, parsley, etc., and place the trimmed bunch in a glass of water in the fridge, loosely covered with a plastic bag. They'll keep for days! Just be sure to change the water once it starts to become discolored.

16. Bake some sweet potatoes. Wrap several sweet potatoes in foil, and bake at 400°F for 30–45 minutes (depending on their size) or until fork-tender all the way through. Having baked sweet potatoes on hand is great for any quick weeknight meal.

17. Make some Riced Cauliflower (p. 176). Having a few side dishes on hand and ready to reheat will make meal prep that much faster during the week.

18. Shred some cabbage, and have it handy for Simply Cole-slaw (p. 202).

19. Have a few bunches of rinsed, torn, and dried kale ready for Kale Chips (p. 170).

20. Make a few meals—such as Family Frittata (p. 164), Chili Verde (p. 104), Chili Colorado (p. 106), Hungarian Stew (p. 100), Fiesta Chicken Soup (p. 102), the stuffing for the Pear and Ground Pork Stuffed Acorn Squash (p. 114), Sloppy Joes (p. 144), Chicken Cacciatore (p. 120), Mini Meatloaves (p. 150), or Spaghetti Squash and Meatballs (p. 148)—to freeze and have on hand for a quick warm-up for fast, already prepared dinners. Taking one day a month to prepare several meals to have in your freezer can make all the difference in the world. One day of extra work equals hours and hours of extra time spent with your family.

What you'll need: *Start to Finish: 30 minutes*

2 pounds ground beef   Shredded cabbage

1 tablespoon ground cumin   Diced avocado

1 tablespoon chili powder   Black olives

1 cup jarred salsa

Brown the ground beef, and season with the spices. Add the salsa, mix well, and heat to simmering. Serve on top of shredded cabbage with diced avocado and black olives.

What you'll need: *Start to Finish: 30 minutes*

2 pounds ground beef   Tomato slices

1½ teaspoons sea salt   Pickle slices

Black pepper   Onion slices

½ tablespoon onion powder   Mayonnaise (P. 62)

½ tablespoon garlic powder   Homemade Ketchup (P. 70)

Lettuce leaves

Mix the beef with the seasonings, form into patties, and fry on a hot griddle or in a skillet for 4 minutes per side. Serve with the suggested condiments.

What you'll need: *Start to Finish: 25 minutes*

2 pounds ground beef   1 (18-ounce) jar sugar-free marinara sauce (Trader Joe's and Bionaturae are great brands)

Sea salt and black pepper

4–5 small zucchini squash, diced

In a large soup pot, brown the ground beef and season with a little sea salt and black pepper. Add the diced zucchini and the marinara sauce. Heat to a simmer, and cook for 5 minutes or until the zucchini is soft but not mushy.

1.
Taco Night

2.
Hamburgers

3.
Easy Meat Sauce

4.
Meatballs in Minutes with a Salad

What you'll need:

Start to Finish: 35 minutes

2 pounds ground beef

1½ teaspoons sea salt

Black pepper

2 teaspoons ground marjoram

2 teaspoons garlic powder

1 egg yolk

<u>Salad</u>

Coconut oil

Salad greens

1 apple, diced

½ cup julienned sun-dried tomatoes

Olive oil and balsamic vinegar

Mix the meatball ingredients, and form into golf ball-sized meatballs. Heat some coconut oil in a large skillet and brown the meatballs on all sides over medium heat. Cover with a lid and let the meatballs steam for 5–6 minutes or until no longer pink in the middle. While the meatballs are steaming, combine the salad ingredients and serve with the meatballs.

5.
Quick Curry Soup

What you'll need:

Start to Finish: 30 minutes

2 pounds ground beef

1 onion, diced

2 tablespoons curry powder (or more to taste)

3 large handfuls baby spinach

1 (13.5-ounce) can coconut milk (Native Forest brand)

3 cups Homemade Chicken Broth (p. 94)

Sea salt and black pepper

In a large soup pot, brown the ground beef and onions. Add the curry powder, and mix well. Add the spinach, pour in the coconut milk and chicken broth, and mix well. Bring to a simmer and stir. Remove the soup from the heat, season with salt and pepper, if desired, and serve.

6.
Chinese Take-Out

What you'll need:

Start to Finish: 35 minutes

2 pounds ground beef

1 tablespoon coconut oil

1 yellow onion, sliced

1½ teaspoons Chinese five-spice powder

½ teaspoon ground ginger

1–2 tablespoons coconut aminos or Bragg Liquid Aminos

1 head green cabbage, shredded

¼ cup Homemade Chicken Broth (p. 94)

In a large skillet or wok, brown the ground beef. Add the coconut oil, onions, five-spice powder, ginger, and coconut aminos, and cook until the onions are soft. Add the cabbage and chicken broth, and cook another 3–4 minutes.

What you'll need:

Start to Finish: 20 minutes

4 precooked chicken breast halves, diced

1 head Romaine lettuce, chopped

4 hard-boiled eggs, diced

1 cup finely chopped broccoli florets

½ cup diced sun-dried tomatoes

¼ cup slivered almonds

1 red bell pepper, diced

Paleo Ranch to taste (p. 64)

Mix all of the ingredients and serve!

What you'll need: *Start to Finish: 15 minutes prep, 5–7 hours cook time*

2 pounds boneless skinless chicken thighs (if you get bone-in, make it 2½–3 pounds)

Sea salt and black pepper to taste

1 yellow onion, sliced

3 garlic cloves, minced

4 carrots, diced

1 cup chicken broth (p. 94)

¼ cup coconut oil, melted

1 tablespoon dried thyme

1 tablespoon rubbed sage

Place the chicken thighs in a slow cooker, and sprinkle with sea salt and black pepper. On top of the chicken, add the onions, garlic, and carrots. In a glass measuring cup, mix together the chicken broth, melted coconut oil, thyme, and sage. Pour this mixture evenly over the chicken and veggies, and cook on high for 5 hours or on low for 7 hours.

(Make this the morning of your busiest day so that you don't have to cook at night.)

What you'll need: *Start to Finish: 35 minutes*

¼ cup coconut oil

2 pounds boneless, skinless chicken thighs or breasts, cut into bite-sized pieces

1 yellow onion, sliced

1 head green cabbage, shredded

2 teaspoons caraway seeds

2 teaspoons paprika

Sea salt and black pepper to taste

In a large soup pot or wok, heat the coconut oil over medium heat, and sauté the chicken thighs and onions until browned. Add the cabbage and spices, and sauté until the cabbage is tender.

7.
Kitchen Sink Chicken Salad

8.
Speedy Slow Cooked Chicken Thighs

9.
Chicken and Cabbage Stir-Fry

SARAH FRAGOSO

10.
Sun-Dried Tomato Chicken Bake

What you'll need:
Start to Finish: 60 minutes

2 pounds boneless, skinless chicken breasts, butterflied

1 (8½-ounce) jar julienned sun-dried tomatoes packed in olive oil

8 garlic cloves, thinly sliced

2 tablespoons dried basil

Sea salt and black pepper to taste

Preheat oven to 375°F. Spread the chicken on the bottom of a large casserole pan. Top evenly with the entire jar of sun-dried tomatoes, garlic, basil, salt, and pepper. Seal tightly with aluminum foil, and bake for 20 minutes. Remove the foil, and bake another 15 minutes or until the chicken is no longer pink in the middle.

11.
Easy Rosemary Chicken

What you'll need:
Start to Finish: 40 minutes

2 tablespoons coconut oil

3 pounds chicken parts (bone in, skin on)

Sea salt and black pepper to taste

1 yellow onion, sliced

5–6 garlic cloves, rough-chopped

4 rosemary sprigs

Juice from half a lemon

½ cup Homemade Chicken Broth (p. 94)

In a large skillet, heat the coconut oil over medium-high heat. Make sure the oil is nice and hot! Season both sides of the chicken pieces with the salt and pepper. Place the chicken in your hot pan with the skin side down, and sear for 5 minutes or until the skin is golden brown. Using tongs, turn the chicken over, and add the onions, garlic, and rosemary sprigs on top of the chicken. Squeeze in the lemon and pour in the chicken broth, cover, and turn down to medium-low heat. Cook another 10–15 minutes or until the chicken is tender and no longer pink in the middle.

12.
Two-Minute Tuna Salad

What you'll need:
Start to Finish: 10 minutes

4 (6-ounce) cans tuna

4 hard-boiled eggs, diced

1 large head red-leaf lettuce (or other lettuce of choice), torn into bite-sized pieces

5 celery stalks, diced

3 tablespoons capers

⅓ cup (or more to taste) Everyday Paleo Vinaigrette (p. 78)

In a large salad bowl, add all of the salad ingredients, top with the vinaigrette, toss well, and serve.

What you'll need:

Start to Finish: 30 minutes

4 tablespoons coconut oil

1 red bell pepper, diced

1 yellow onion, diced

2 pounds wild-caught shrimp, peeled, deveined, and tails removed (Try to find frozen shrimp, already cleaned, for fast prep. Trader Joe's often carries wild-caught shrimp that have been peeled, deveined, and tails removed.)

5 giant handfuls baby spinach leaves

4 tablespoons full-fat canned coconut milk

1 tablespoon curry powder or more to taste

Sea salt and black pepper to taste

In a large skillet, heat the coconut oil over medium heat. Add the bell peppers and onions and cook until tender, about 4–5 minutes. Add the shrimp and cook, tossing frequently, for 2–3 minutes or until the shrimp is pink. Add the spinach, coconut milk, and seasonings. Mix well until warm and the spinach wilts. Serve.

What you'll need: *Start to Finish: 20 minutes prep, 5–6 hours cook time*

Dry rub

3 tablespoons chili powder

1 teaspoon ground coriander

2 teaspoons ground cumin

2 teaspoons onion powder

1 tablespoon dried parsley

¼ teaspoon chipotle powder

2 teaspoons sea salt

Pork

4- to 5-pound pork butt roast

2 yellow onions, sliced

Mix the dry rub ingredients in a small bowl. Rub the entire roast with the dry rub (use it all). Place a layer of sliced onions on the bottom of your slow cooker. Place the roast on top. Put the rest of the sliced onions on top of the roast. (No liquid is necessary.) Cook the roast on high for 5–6 hours, and turn it down to low for another 3–4 hours or until the roast is falling apart and easy to shred.

What you'll need:

Start to Finish: 30 minutes

4 pork chops, ¼-inch thick

Sea salt and black pepper

½ cup Dijon mustard

1 teaspoon mustard powder

1 teaspoon dried thyme

1 teaspoon crushed garlic

1 tablespoon coconut oil

Preheat your oven to 425°F. Season the pork chops lightly with salt and pepper. In a small bowl, combine the mustard, mustard powder, thyme, and garlic; mix well. Spread the mustard sauce evenly over both sides of the chops. Heat the oil in a large ovenproof skillet over medium-high heat. Add the chops, and brown for 2 minutes per side. Transfer the skillet to the oven, and cook for an additional 5–8 minutes until the chops are no longer pink and cooked through. Serve over sautéed baby spinach.

13.
Fast Shrimp

14.
Beyond-Easy Pulled Pork

15.
Dad's Pork Chops

What Sarah Wants You to Have and Where to Find It

In Your Pantry ➡

Coconut milk	*Native Forest Brand, Thai Kitchen Organic, or Chaokoh (found at most major grocery stores, health food stores, or online at Amazon.com)*
Organic diced tomatoes	*Bionaturae.com or TropicalTraditions.com*
Organic tomato paste	*Bionaturae.com or TropicalTraditions.com*
Chicken broth	*Make your own (found on page 94) or purchase a gluten-free, organic, free-range option found at most major grocery stores, Trader Joe's, or health food stores*
Coconut flakes	*TropicalTraditions.com*
Coconut flour	*TropicalTraditions.com*
Almond meal	*AmminNut.com, Trader Joe's*
Raw almonds	*AmminNut.com, Trader Joe's*
Raw pecans	*Most major grocery stores or health food stores*
Raw walnuts	*Found in most major grocery stores*
Almond butter	*AmminNut.com*
Beef jerky	*StevesOriginal.com or PaleoBrands.com*
Canned wild-caught salmon	*Found at Costco, Trader Joe's or online at WildPlanetFoods.com*
Canned wild-caught tuna	*WildPlanetFoods.com*
Olives	*Most major grocery stores or health food stores*
Artichoke hearts	*Most major grocery stores or health food stores*
Dried unsweetened fruit	*Trader Joe's, health food stores, online at BellaViva.com*
Extra-virgin olive oil	*All major grocery or health food stores, and online at Bionaturae.com or TropicalTraditions.com*
Coconut oil	*TropicalTraditions.com*
El Pato hot sauce and El Pato enchilada sauce	*At most major grocery stores*
Jalapeños	*Most major grocery stores or health food stores*
Canned diced green chilies	*Most major grocery stores*
Sun-dried tomatoes	*Costco, all major grocery stores, Trader Joe's, health food stores, or online at Bionaturae.com, TropicalTraditions.com, Mooneyfarms.com*
As many spices as you can get your hands on!	*With spices you never have an excuse to eat a boring meal! Penzeys.com or SimplyOrganic.com, or save money and keep your spices fresh and try to buy in bulk, often offered at Whole Foods and other health food stores.*

Eggs	*Preferably free range (not fed soy) or omega-3 enriched, found on line at GrassFedTraditions.com*
Grass-fed ground beef	*GrassLandBeef.com, GrassFedTraditions.com, TXBarOrganics.com, EatWild.com*
Free-range chicken	*GrassLandBeef.com, GrassFedTraditions.com, EatWild.com*
Deli meat	*AppleateFarms.com*
Bacon	*ApplegateFarms.com, NimanRanch.com, EatWild.com, GrassLandBeef.com*
Mustard	*Annies.com or Trader Joe's Brand, or any gluten-free mustards found in most major grocery stores*
Salsa	*Found in most major grocery stores*
Mayonnaise	*Found on (p. 62)*
Hot sauce	*Tapatio, Sriracha, or any other hot sauce that is gluten and sugar-free*
Chili oil	*Found in the ethnic food isle of most major grocery stores*
Fish sauce	*RedBoatFishSauce.com*
Thai curry paste	*Thai Kitchen found at most major grocery stores or online at Amazon.com*
Broccoli	*Found in most major grocery stores*
Spinach	*Found in most major grocery stores*
Kale	*Found in most major grocery stores*
Carrots	*Found in most major grocery stores*
Cucumber	*Found in most major grocery stores*
Organic lettuce mix	*Found in most major grocery stores*
Romaine lettuce	*Found in most major grocery stores*
Onions	*Found in most major grocery stores*
Garlic	*Found in most major grocery stores*
Apples	*Found in most major grocery stores*
Blueberries	*Found in most major grocery stores*
Limes	*Found in most major grocery stores*
Any veggie and fruit that you can get your hands on that is as fresh as possible and in season!	*To find a local CSA or farmers market visit LocalHarvest.org*

In Your Fridge

One-Week Meal Plan

Below you will find a *suggested* one-week meal plan with easy-to-prepare recipes. I designed the meal plan to feed the average family of four or five people, but every family is different. If you have three growing teenage boys, it might not be enough food, and if you have two small toddlers, it might be too much. For kids, you might also need to add more fat and carbs to the meals to keep them full and energized, so feel free to adjust by adding in additional sweet potatoes, winter squash, or other starchier vegetables, and of course plenty of protein! As you will see below, I suggest that you rely heavily on leftovers as you go through your week, so make sure to adjust your shopping lists if you need to double a recipe.

Furthermore, I did not include snacks into the meal plan, but please snack if you need to—children especially will likely need and want to have snacks in between meals! For the grownups, when you eat plenty of fat and protein during meals, the need to snack diminishes and you stay full for longer durations. Suggested snack options include beef jerky, hardboiled eggs, leftovers, sliced veggies and Paleo ranch or guacamole, berries, sliced chicken, sliced steak, olives, artichoke hearts, cauliflower hummus, meatballs, mini meatloaves, etc. I suggest that when you do snack, there is protein involved and not just fruit or veggies.

Things to do ahead of time to help prepare you for this week of meals:

Make:

- **Mayonnaise (p. 62)**

- **Everyday Paleo Ranch (p. 64)**

- **Homemade Ketchup (p. 70)**

- **Homemade Chicken Broth (p. 94)**

- **Cilantro Pesto (p. 68)**

Breakfast:	Family Frittata (p. 164)	**Day 1**
Lunch:	Two-Minute Tuna Salad (p. 46)	
Dinner:	Spaghetti Squash and Meatballs (p. 148)	
Breakfast:	Leftover Family Frittata	**Day 2**
Lunch:	Leftover Spaghetti Squash and Meatballs	
Dinner:	Sun Dried Tomato Chicken Bake (p. 46), big green salad with Everyday Paleo Ranch (p. 64)	
Breakfast:	Winter Squash Hash and Eggs (p. 160)	**Day 3**
Lunch:	Leftover Sun-Dried Tomato Chicken Bake, or Egg Salad (p. 166) with sliced veggies	
Dinner:	Beyond Easy Pulled Pork (p. 47), and Roasted Beet Salad (p. 180)	
Breakfast:	Leftover Beyond Easy Pulled Pork with fried or poached eggs	**Day 4**
Lunch:	Vietnamese Lamb Lettuce Wraps (p. 154)	
Dinner:	Mini Meatloaves (p. 150), Sweet Potato Chips (p. 172), and Zucchini Salad (p. 184)	
Breakfast:	Creamy Breakfast Quiche (p. 162)	**Day 5**
Lunch:	Tuna Stuffed Eggs (p. 166)	
Dinner:	Slow Chicken Curry (p. 88) and Riced Cauliflower (p. 176)	
Breakfast:	Leftover Creamy Breakfast Quiche	**Day 6**
Lunch:	Left over Slow Chicken Curry and Riced Cauliflower	
Dinner:	Taco Night (p. 43)	
Breakfast:	Pesto Baked Eggs (p. 158)	**Day 7**
Lunch:	Left over Taco Night or Turkey "Sushi" Rolls (p. 174)	
Dinner:	One Pot Chicken Drumsticks (p. 124) and Poblano Roasted Sweet Potatoes (p. 182)	

Shopping List for One-Week Meal Plan

This shopping list includes the staple ingredients for the suggested one-week meal plan, but it does not include the ingredients to the items that I suggest you prepare ahead of time, such as the mayonnaise, Paleo ranch, ketchup, and chicken broth. As suggested in the beginning of the meal plan, you may need more or less than what's suggested based on the needs of your family. This list is simply a guideline to help you get started with your weekly planning and preparation!

- Baby arugula—enough for 5 cups
- Fresh basil—enough for 3½ cups
- 1 head green cabbage
- 1 poblano pepper
- 1 large tomato
- 3 avocados
- 1 large bunch of baby spinach
- Spinach leaves—enough for 1 cup
- 1 head cauliflower
- 1 large bunch bok choy
- 2 large cucumbers
- 1 red or yellow bell pepper
- 1 bunch Italian flat leaf parsley
- 1 bunch fresh dill
- 1 bunch cilantro
- 1 bunch of large red beets
- 1 bunch green onions
- 5 small carrots
- 7 small zucchini
- 1 small sweet potato
- 4 large sweet potatoes
- 1 large head red leaf lettuce (for Two-Minute Tuna Salad)
- 1 large head green leaf lettuce (for big green salad on Day 2)
- 2 heads celery
- 1 large spaghetti squash
- 1 small butternut squash
- 1 medium white onion
- 4 small yellow onions
- 1 medium yellow onion
- 3 small red onions
- Chives
- ½ pound crimini mushrooms or enough to make 2½ cups diced

- 4 bulbs garlic
- Additional veggies for slicing, such as bell peppers, carrots, cucumbers, etc.
- 4 limes
- 3 lemons

- 2 pounds boneless, skinless chicken breasts
- 2 pounds boneless, skinless chicken thighs
- 8 chicken drumsticks
- 5 dozen eggs
- 2 pounds ground lamb
- 4 pounds ground beef
- 2 pounds thick cut bacon
- 4-5-pound pork butt roast
- 2 pounds ground pork
- ½ pound turkey deli meat
- 2 ham steaks or 1 ham steak and 1 package of prosciutto
- 5 (6-ounce) cans tuna

- Fresh orange juice

- Coconut Aminos or Bragg Liquid Aminos
- Sesame oil
- 1 jar of salsa
- 2-3 (2¼-ounce) cans sliced black olives
- 2 (8½-ounce) jars julienned sun-dried tomatoes packed in olive oil
- 2 (13½-ounce) cans full-fat coconut milk (Native Forest Brand)
- 1 (32-ounce) box chicken broth (unless you make homemade)

- 1 small jar of capers
- 1 small jar kalamata olives
- 1 jar dill pickles (Bubbies brand if possible)
- 1 (24-ounce) jar of strained tomatoes (Bionaturae brand) or tomato sauce
- 1 (6-ounce) jar tomato paste
- Fish sauce
- Sriracha sauce
- Walnut halves—enough for ½ cups
- Sesame seeds
- Dijon mustard
- Red wine vinegar
- Extra-virgin olive oil
- Coconut oil

- Dried Parsley
- Curry powder
- Chili powder
- Ground coriander
- Ground cumin
- Ground cinnamon
- Onion powder
- Chipotle powder
- Italian seasoning
- Basil
- Oregano
- Poultry seasoning
- Paprika
- Rubbed sage
- Sea salt
- Black pepper

Budget Guide

One of the most frequent questions I hear from families is, "How do you eat Paleo on a budget?" Below I include some suggestions that should help you answer that question, as well as dispel some of the myths that seem to hover around the cost of eating a healthier diet.

1. Plan, plan, plan ahead! Have you ever shopped for groceries when hungry, without a list or without purpose? Bad idea. The same is true for when you head out to go shopping for your Paleo ingredients. Do not go to the store without a list or plan, and never shop on an empty stomach! If you go to the store without purpose, you're likely to come home with a hodgepodge of ingredients with no rhyme or reason. Especially when you are brand new to this lifestyle, this can be an extremely frustrating and expensive experience! I can't stress enough the importance of putting at least a little bit of thought into your weekly meals before you make your venture to the market. For example, I have clients who come to me complaining that they have giant roasts and racks of ribs in their fridge that are growing green with mold because they haven't had the time to cook them! Well, roasts and ribs take time and cost more money than ground beef or chicken thighs, and although roasts and ribs are awesome and delicious, without a plan for what to do with these cuts of meat, they are likely to go to waste or die of freezer burn before you get the chance to make them into something delicious. The moral of the story is this; look ahead at your week and plan accordingly. If you know you have deadlines and baseball

Plan, Plan, Plan...

games every night of the week, go for three slow cooker meals that can be made into leftovers the next day and a couple of simple-to-make meals like Taco Night (p. 43) or Easy Rosemary Chicken (p. 46). Save the roasts or ribs for weeks when your schedule is less demanding. Any wasted food is money down the drain, and if your freezer is filled with hard-to-make cuts of meat, you are more likely to not only spend more money on groceries, but also give up on cooking and default to eating out!

2. Freeze that food! Make twice the amount that you will need for dinner and freeze the leftovers for busy nights. How does this save money? It's like insurance. You might spend a little more at first, but a huge part of budgeting is avoiding sporadic visits to the grocery store or calling the nearest take-out joint. Always have food on hand, whether it's frozen and ready for a quick warm-up or if it's ingredients for an easy-to-make meal. Without this food insurance, you are sure to see your food bill go up.

3. Be committed. I noticed that initially we spent a bit more on our monthly food bill, but I also noticed that over time we actually spent less because we were committed to eating at home and committed to eating as Paleo as possible! Before eating Paleo, I would do my normal weekly grocery shopping, get lazy, and eat out the majority of the week. This would leave me with a fridge full of wilted veggies and expired meat that I would have to throw out, and then I would repeat the vicious cycle. Also, I would inevitably visit the coffee shop drive-through at least once a day to fill up on a sugary caffeine treat, and holy cow do those drinks add up! Especially when you take into account the additional smoothies or hot chocolate drinks I would buy for the kids. Furthermore, what about those absentminded trips to the drive-through to get the kids a quick meal or snack! Say goodbye to those and say hello to more money in your bank account. Be committed to not eating out during the week and kick the coffee latte habit and you'll be funding the entire block's college fund before you know it.

4. This is not something that you can plan for, but it's worth taking into account when considering the overall cost of living a healthier lifestyle—you'll save money on medical

and health care expenses! I can't tell you how many people have told me about the lists upon lists of medications that they were able to stop taking thanks to simply changing their nutrition. Think about the average amount of money most people spend on medications and doctor's visits, and put that right into your savings account. The average American fills twelve prescriptions per year, and that's just the average! If you are not on medications, think about the fact that you probably would be someday if not for your commitment to a healthier lifestyle. Not a single member of our family has had to visit a doctor this year, which has saved us thousands of dollars in co-insurance payments and prescriptions. Being healthy equals money in the bank.

5. Get critical of how you spend your money. Living a Paleo lifestyle has made us become more aware of how we can simplify our lives in other areas. I already talked about how we no longer have cable—hello to an average savings of $200 dollars a month! Goodbye old sugary coffee habit, $150 a month saved. We have committed to not eating out at all during the week, which we used to do three or four times, resulting in an average of $210 a week saved. We decided to put away a certain amount of money every week into our saving account, and if we run out of our allotted spending money, we don't have any money to play with! We learned fast what we could and could not get away with as we watched our health improve and our savings account grow. Another tip to help you save—drink less! We used to drink an average of one to two glasses of wine a night each. Now we indulge now and then on the weekends, and our health and pocketbooks have both improved. Cutting back on the booze has saved us an average of $50 a week. Another way we save money is by choosing to do activities outside that are free, and we spend less time doing activities that cost money! With just these few simple and mindful changes, we are currently saving an average of $1400 a month!

6. Join a CSA. To find a CSA near you visit www.localharvest. org. What is a CSA? CSA stands for Community Supported Agriculture, and joining one is a wonderful way to have a year-round supply of farm-fresh vegetables. When

you join a CSA, you purchase a membership that entitles you to a box or set amount of seasonal produce, straight from the actual farm. The price of joining a CSA is different depending on where you live, but the budgeting advantages are many. With my own experience with joining a CSA I have noticed the following rewards, which has done wonders for our grocery expenses:

- By having a set amount of vegetables each week, I avoid over-buying or splurging on other items that I might find if I went to the store or the farmers market.

- I do not go to the store as often because I make my one trip to the farm at the beginning of the week, and then try to build my meals around what's in my CSA share. Having a well-stocked freezer full of meat helps in this area as well. The less you have to go to the grocery store, the more money you are bound to save by avoiding impulse or splurge purchases.

- I'm more likely to stick to my commitment to cook because I feel invested in my CSA, and I hate to see the amazingly fresh vegetables go to waste. By having a relationship with the people who work so hard to grow my food, I feel a part of the deal is that I make sure to eat what I receive each week!

- Throughout the week, I save on gas by making one trip to the CSA instead of multiple trips to the store.

7. Buy meat in bulk. This is a very similar concept to joining a CSA. By purchasing meat in bulk, you might pay a bit more up front, but you will save a tremendous amount of money down the line. Most of the time you will actually pay less per pound by purchasing a half or a quarter of an animal than you would if you just purchased meat as needed from the grocery store. Also, by having meat in your freezer, you are never faced with what to have for dinner. When you buy meat in bulk and you're also a part of a CSA, it's a serious recipe for success and money saving. You can plan your meals around what cuts of meat you have available, along

with your weekly supply of vegetables, and it really simplifies life. You can share a cow with friends, which also helps with cost. We do this a couple of times a year, and having a freezer full of meat is about the best and most stress-free feeling a Paleo family can have! To find local sources for grass-fed meat that you can purchase in bulk, visit www.eatwild.com

8. Make your own condiments and dressings! By following the first section of recipes in this book, you'll find that making your own condiments can be a huge money saver! Condiments and dressings are expensive, and it's difficult to find ones that are not laden with vegetable oils and unnecessary fillers or sweeteners. Every couple of weeks, make the salad dressings, mayonnaise, and sauces, and you'll have plenty of flavorful options to pair with your basket of vegetables from your CSA and your freezer full of meat from your cow share.

9. Get as many meals as you can out of one recipe! For example, roast a chicken and eat it, and then boil the carcass. You'll be surprised at all the meat that comes off of what's remaining, which can be used to make soup. Strain the broth for your chicken stock. Save your beef bones to make bone broth, and save vegetables scraps to make soup or stock with. Living a natural paleo lifestyle does not have to mean breaking the bank, and hopefully these budgeting tips will help you make the leap to the path of penny pinching Paleo success!

RECIPES

Now, it's time for the food!
Use your imagination, and let your creativity run wild. Make these recipes as suggested, or tweak them to fit the tastes and needs of your family. Most important, enjoy the time spent cooking with your family, and have fun!

Sauces and Dips

Slow Cooker Recipes

Soups and Stews

Meaty Meals

Sides, Salads and Small Plates

Fruity Creations and Treats

Sauces and Dips

Mayonnaise

2 egg yolks

2 tablespoons apple cider vinegar

I teaspoon yellow mustard

I teaspoon sea salt

¼ teaspoon cayenne pepper

2 cups light olive oil or walnut oil

Prep Time:
15 minutes

1. Using either a hand-held mixer, food processor, or a blender that does not get too hot, add the eggs yolks, vinegar, mustard, sea salt, and cayenne pepper and blend together for five seconds.

2. Leave the blender or hand-held mixer running and slowly, slowly, slowly, drop by drop or in a very slow drizzle, add the oil. Be patient. Do not dump all the oil in quickly and give up!!

3. When the mixture begins to emulsify, or thicken, only then can you be a bit faster about pouring in the oil, but still take your time. If you see your mayo start to turn grainy, or separate, stop the blender. Turn the blender or hand-held mixer off once all the oil is in and the mayonnaise is thickened to your desired consistency. Do not use a Vitamix blender because it will make the mayonnaise too hot and it will not emulsify. You can also make mayonnaise by hand by using either a whisk (a great way to get in a quick workout and fun to do with a partner or child) or a hand-held stick blender like this one: http://www.zappos.com/multiview/7831553/62983. Makes approximately 2½ cups of mayonnaise.

TIP! Do not throw away your mayonnaise mixture if it doesn't work or if the oil separates from too much blending. Simply take another egg yolk and tablespoon of vinegar, whisk those two ingredients together, and slowly whisk or blend back in the original "messed up" mayonnaise. Remember, a slow pour is the secret to success, and stop blending once you reach your desired mayo consistency.

Something Extra: *This is a super-fun project for those of you with or without kids. It's also a science project—and a lesson in emulsification and how two different agents "suspend" together that would not normally mix! Do an Internet search on emulsions and learn together how it works; then make your mayonnaise in the kitchen and observe the magic happen.*

Everyday Paleo Ranch

½ cup Mayonnaise (p. 62)

1 tablespoon full-fat canned coconut milk (Native Forest brand)

1 teaspoon dried dill

½ teaspoon dried parsley

¼ teaspoon minced garlic

Black pepper

Prep Time:
10 minutes

Gently stir all ingredients together and serve as a dressing for salads or a dip for veggies, sliced chicken breasts, or anything else you might want to dip. Makes approximately ½ a cup of Everyday Paleo Ranch.

Something Extra: *Kids historically love Ranch dressing. This one tastes just about as close to the "real deal" as you can get, and it actually is made from real food! Let your kids whisk the ingredients together and introduce new veggies by having a sample tray on your dinner table. A good way to try new foods without making them scary or uninviting is to have a plate of finger foods that anyone is free to sample. Place a bowl of Everyday Paleo Ranch on the table and surround it with different types of olives, celery sticks, carrot sticks, cucumber slices, and small pieces of broccoli and cauliflower. Artichoke hearts are a great addition to any meal, and strips of bell peppers are also delicious dipped in Everyday Paleo Ranch.*

Everyday Paleo Caesar Salad Dressing

3 tablespoons Mayonnaise (p. 62)

½ cup extra-virgin olive oil

1 tablespoon lemon juice

1 teaspoon minced garlic

½ teaspoon Dijon mustard

1 tablespoon minced anchovy filets (optional)

Sea salt and black pepper (you won't need much, or any, salt if you do use the anchovy filets, so taste the dressing before you add any salt)

Prep Time:
15 minutes

Whisk all of the ingredients together and serve over Romaine lettuce with additional anchovy filets if desired. Makes approximately 1 cup dressing.

Something Extra: *We all love Caesar salad, and there's no reason to not enjoy the flavors of this popular dressing, minus the cheese and croutons! Three of us in my family love anchovies and two do not, so we split the dressing in half, and those who like anchovies whisk the minced filets into their portion and those who don't add a little more sea salt, and everyone is happy! Have your kids tear apart the lettuce leaves and help you whisk the dressing.*

Curry Spread

½ cup Mayonnaise (p. 62)

I teaspoon curry powder

½ teaspoon paprika

Prep Time:
5 minutes

Stir the mayo and spices together. This is delicious on my Curry Burgers (p. 146) or as a dip for veggies or a sauce for your favorite protein.

Cilantro Pesto

½ cup walnuts (soaked overnight in water and drained)

I–2 garlic cloves

½ cup olive oil

Juice from ½ a lemon

½ teaspoon sea salt

3 cups or I large bunch cilantro, stems removed

Prep Time:
5 minutes

Place all the ingredients in a food processor and blend until smooth.

Serve with the Mexican Beef Skewers (p. 152) or anything else, from eggs to veggies; this pesto is fresh and delightful! Makes approximately I½ cups pesto.

Chipotle Cream Sauce

¼ cup full-fat canned coconut milk (Native Forest Brand)

2 tablespoons tomato paste (Bionaturae brand)

⅛ teaspoon chipotle powder

½ teaspoon ground cumin

¼ teaspoon sea salt

I garlic clove

Prep Time:
10 minutes

Put all the ingredients into a blender or food processor and blend until the garlic is completely processed and the sauce is smooth.

Serve as a dipping sauce for the Mexican Beef Skewers (p. 152) along with Cilantro Pesto (above).

Homemade Ketchup

1 tablespoon coconut oil

¼ cup minced white onion

2 garlic cloves, minced

7 ounces organic tomato paste
(Bionaturae brand)

1 tablespoon apple cider vinegar

1 tablespoon balsamic vinegar

1 teaspoon yellow mustard

1 teaspoon sea salt

1 teaspoon smoked paprika

½ teaspoon celery seed

1 ½ teaspoons chili powder

¼ cup apple juice

Prep Time:
25 minutes

Cook Time:
10 minutes

1. In a medium skillet, melt the coconut oil over medium heat and cook the minced onions until they become translucent.

2. Add the garlic and sauté just until fragrant.

3. Add to the skillet the remaining ingredients and whisk together. Bring the mixture to a simmer, turn heat to low, and cook for an additional 5 minutes, stirring often.

4. Remove from the heat and let the ketchup cool down before storing it in a glass container. Makes approximately 2 cups ketchup.

Something Extra: *Most kids—well, most people—love ketchup, but most ketchups are filled with high-fructose corn syrup and preservatives and leave something to be desired as a healthy choice for a condiment. Not this one! With this ketchup you can feel good about slathering it on top of bun-less burgers or my Mini Meatloaves (p. 150). Have the kids help you whisk and taste along the way.*

Spicy Sriracha Mayo

½ cup Mayonnaise (p. 62)

2 teaspoons Sriracha sauce

Prep Time:
5 minutes

Mix together and serve with my Seared Ahi or Salmon (p. 134) or with any fish or chicken dish. Spicy and delicious! Adjust the amount of Sriracha sauce based on your taste.

Garlic Lemon Aioli

½ cup Mayonnaise (p. 62)

Juice from ½ a lemon

1 garlic clove, finely minced

¼ teaspoon black pepper

Prep Time:
5 minutes

Stir all the ingredients together and serve with the Smoked Salmon and Poached Egg Salad (p. 142) or the Tuna Patties (p. 136). This is a great accompaniment to any seafood dish or salad.

Brother Mark BBQ Sauce

6 garlic cloves, minced

½ yellow onion, diced

3 tablespoons coconut oil or bacon grease

2 teaspoons lemon zest

1 small sprig rosemary

1 cup pineapple juice

1 cup apple juice

½ cup organic tomato paste (Bionaturae brand)

¼ cup red wine

1 tablespoon coconut aminos or Bragg Liquid Aminos

1 teaspoon sea salt

½ tablespoon paprika

1 tablespoon chili powder

½ tablespoon ground cumin

⅛ teaspoon cayenne

⅛ teaspoon red chili flakes

1 teaspoon Dijon mustard

1 tablespoon apple cider vinegar

¼ cup water

Prep Time:
40 minutes

Cook Time:
30 minutes

1. Over medium heat in a medium skillet, sauté the garlic and onions in 2 tablespoons of the coconut oil or bacon grease until the onions are translucent.

2. Add the lemon zest, rosemary sprig, ⅛ cup of the pineapple juice, and ⅛ cup of the apple juice to the onion and garlic mixture and bring to a simmer; then turn heat down to low and simmer while you continue to prepare the sauce.

3. While the onion mixture is simmering, in a separate large skillet heat the remaining tablespoon of coconut oil over medium-low heat and whisk in the tomato paste.

4. Turn the heat up to medium to medium-high and slowly add the wine as well as the remaining pineapple and apple juice, ¼ cup at a time, stirring constantly.

5. Strain the liquid from the onion-and-rosemary mixture pan through a sieve or strainer into the tomato sauce mixture and let the sauce cook down and thicken while stirring constantly over medium to medium-high heat (approximately 7–10 minutes.)

6. Add the remaining ingredients, whisk together well, and simmer for another 7–10 minutes. Makes approximately 2 cups BBQ sauce.

Something Extra: *My older brother Mark and I have been cooking together since we were kids, and Mark played a huge part in my effort to finish this cookbook. My brother is such an inspiration to me. From him I learned to be strong and to stand up for what I believe in, to be brave, to fight when I need to and to love fiercely, to be honest and not hide what I'm feeling, to be kind to everyone and to help people in need, to cry when I'm sad, to hug my friends and family, and to not say sorry if I haven't done anything wrong, but when I am wrong, to fess up and apologize right away. Thank you Mark for being my brother and for sharing your heart and soul with the world. This is Brother Mark's BBQ sauce, which we tweaked and tested and tried again and again until it was perfect. I promise you this sauce will make you want to hug my brother; it's that good.*

Korean BBQ Sauce

½ yellow onion, diced

I teaspoon lemon zest

I small sprig fresh rosemary

6 garlic cloves, minced

¼ cup plus 2 tablespoons pineapple juice

¼ cup plus 2 tablespoons water

2 fresh jalapeños, deseeded and sliced

2 tablespoons chopped fresh ginger

4 tablespoon chopped fresh basil

I tablespoon sesame oil

½ cup tomato paste (Bionaturae brand)

¾ cup pineapple juice mixed with ¾ cup apple juice

4 tablespoons coconut aminos or Bragg Liquid Aminos

I tablespoon apple cider vinegar

½ tablespoon paprika

⅛ teaspoon cayenne pepper

¼ teaspoon sea salt

¼ teaspoon black pepper

Prep Time:
40 minutes

Cook Time:
30 minutes

1. In a medium skillet over medium heat, add the onions, lemon zest, rosemary sprig, minced garlic, pineapple juice, water, sliced jalapeños, ginger, and basil.

2. Bring to a boil; then turn the heat down to low and bring the mixture to a simmer. Let it simmer while you continue the sauce preparation.

3. Meanwhile in a separate medium skillet add the sesame oil and heat over medium heat and whisk in the tomato paste.

4. Slowly add the pineapple-and-apple juice mixture ¼ cup at a time, whisking constantly.

5. Pour the liquid contents of the skillet containing the onion and rosemary mixture through a sieve or strainer into the tomato mixture and whisk together.

6. Add the remaining ingredients, stir well, and let simmer another 7–10 minutes. Makes approximately 2 cups BBQ sauce.

Something Extra: *This is another rendition of Brother Mark BBQ Sauce, but with Asian inspiration. It was made to be paired with the Brined and Sauced Baby Back Ribs (p. 110), but it can also be used on grilled chicken or any other protein of your choice that you think might need a little extra love.*

Everyday Paleo Vinaigrette

2 teaspoons Dijon mustard

¼ cup red wine vinegar

½ cup extra-virgin olive oil

2 tablespoons fresh orange juice

1 tablespoon dried parsley

Prep Time:
10 minutes

Whisk all ingredients together and serve with your favorite salad.

This dressing is amazing paired with the Roasted Beet Salad (p. 180).

Balsamic Vinaigrette

3 tablespoons extra-virgin olive oil

2 tablespoons balsamic vinegar

1 tablespoon spicy brown mustard

1 tablespoon minced fresh dill

Sea salt and black pepper to taste

Prep Time:
10 minutes

Whisk all ingredients together and serve with your favorite salad.

I recommend this dressing on the Chopped Broccoli Salad (p. 178).

Cauliflower Hummus

4 cups steamed cauliflower

2 tablespoons almond butter

¼ cup extra-virgin olive oil

1–2 garlic cloves

1 teaspoon ground cumin

½ teaspoon paprika

Pinch cayenne pepper

½ teaspoon sea salt

Prep Time:
25 minutes

1. To steam the cauliflower, place the cauliflower florets into a steamer basket in a large pot and add water just until it hits the bottom of the steamer basket.

2. Cover with a lid and bring the water to a boil. Turn the heat down to low or medium-low and steam for 6 minutes or until fork-tender.

3. Remove the florets immediately and let them cool.

4. Once the cauliflower is cool, place the steamed florets into a food processor along with the remaining ingredients and process until completely smooth. Serve with raw veggies, olives, and even slices of cooked chicken breast for dipping. Makes approximately 4 cups hummus.

Something Extra: *I love hummus, and my husband, John, gave me the idea of creating one of my favorite dips with cauliflower instead of chickpeas. Cauliflower is so useful and versatile; this hummus is now one of our go-to snacks and a great addition to the kids' lunch boxes. My boys like sliced jicama and carrot sticks with this dip. Let each member of your family decide what they want to dip, and have fun exploring new possibilities.*

Slow Cooker Recipes

Pork Green Curry

1 tablespoon coconut oil

2 pounds pork loin, cut into bite-sized pieces

3 teaspoons Chinese five-spice powder

1 (13.5-ounce) can full-fat coconut milk (Native Forest brand)

2 tablespoons green curry paste or more if you like it spicy (Thai Kitchen brand)

1/3 cup Homemade Chicken Broth (p. 94)

2 tablespoons fish sauce (www.RedBoatFishSauce.com)

10 asparagus spears, cut into bite-sized pieces

1 orange, red, or yellow bell pepper, cut into bite-sized pieces

1 small yellow onion, chopped

Fresh basil for garnish

1. Heat the coconut oil in a large skillet over medium heat.

2. While the oil is heating, place the pieces of cut-up pork loin in a medium bowl and add the Chinese five-spice powder. Toss the pork pieces with the spices until all are coated.

3. Add the spiced pork to the hot oil and cook for 3–4 minutes, stirring often until all of the pieces are browned.

4. Remove the seared pork pieces from the skillet and put them into the slow cooker.

5. Add the coconut milk to the skillet that the pork was cooking in; make sure the pan is hot enough that the coconut milk sizzles as you pour it in.

6. Add the chicken broth, curry paste, and fish sauce to the coconut milk and whisk together, making sure to scrape up any pork bits and spices as you whisk.

7. Bring to a boil and let the sauce simmer for 3–4 minutes.

8. Pour the sauce over the pork that's in the slow cooker, add the vegetables, and cook on low for 4–6 hours. Serve garnished with chopped fresh basil or cilantro.

Prep Time:
30 minutes

Cook Time:
4–6 hours

Serves:
4–5

Something Extra: *This meal is delicious with Riced Cauliflower (p. 176). My family also enjoys this dish prepared with red curry paste rather than green for some variation of flavor and a bit more spice. Take advantage of slow cooker nights to spend more time with your family. Play a board game after dinner, take a walk, or even work out together! Try to make the night a NO TV night. Instead, reconnect with those you love.*

Family-Style Short Ribs

2 tablespoons coconut oil

5–6 pounds beef short ribs

Sea salt and black pepper

2 cups Brother Mark BBQ Sauce (p. 74)

Prep Time:
15 minutes

Cook Time:
8–9 hours (low)
4–6 hours (high)

Serves:
4–5

1. Heat the coconut oil in a large skillet over medium to medium-high heat.

2. While the oil is heating, season the short ribs generously with salt and pepper.

3. Sear the ribs in the hot oil for 3–4 minutes per side or until browned and crisp on the outside.

4. Place the seared ribs in a slow cooker, cover with 2 cups of Brother Mark BBQ Sauce, and cook on low for 8–9 hours (low) or 4–5 hours (high), or until the meat is falling off the bone.

Something Extra: *Short ribs in my house are total comfort food, especially when slathered with delicious BBQ sauce and cooked all day, low and slow. There is really nothing better than coming home to a house filled with the delicious smell of what I can only describe as warmth and love. Yes, it sounds sappy, but fall-off-the-bone meat chunks make me feel sentimental. (It must be the cave girl in me.) Be sure to save the bones from these ribs to make bone broth; simply follow the directions of Homemade Chicken Broth (p. 94), substituting roasted or slow cooked beef bones for the chicken bones.*

Slow Chicken Curry

2 tablespoons curry powder

1 tablespoon paprika

2 teaspoons sea salt

1 teaspoon black pepper

2 pounds boneless, skinless chicken thighs

4 garlic cloves, minced

1 yellow onion, sliced

3 carrots, diced

4 celery stalks, diced

1 cup full-fat canned coconut milk (Native Forest brand)

1 cup Homemade Chicken Broth (p. 94)

Prep Time:
30 minutes

Cook Time:
4–7 hours

Serves:
5–6

1. In a small bowl, mix all of the dry spices together.

2. Place the chicken thighs in a slow cooker and pour the spice mixture over the chicken thighs and toss together until all the thighs are coated with the spices.

3. Sprinkle on the minced garlic and add the onions, carrots, and celery.

4. In a small mixing bowl, whisk together the coconut milk and the chicken broth.

5. Pour the coconut milk and chicken broth mixture over the top of the chicken and vegetables and cook on high in the slow cooker for 4 hours or on low for 6–7 hours.

Something Extra: *After a long day, there's nothing better than coming home to dinner already prepared! I know this slow cooker recipe is a winner because it's the recipe that I demonstrate and serve to people who attend my Everyday Paleo Workshops, and this dish is always well received. It's another meal that pairs well with Riced Cauliflower (p. 176). We also like to make Chopped Salad (p. 198) to eat with my Slow Chicken Curry.*

Slow Cooker Lamb Shank

3 tablespoons coconut oil

4–5 small lamb shanks

Sea salt and black pepper

1 yellow onion, sliced

5 garlic cloves, roughly chopped

2 cups tomato sauce or strained tomatoes (Bionaturae brand)

3/8 cup peach or apricot preserves (no-sugar-added)

1 teaspoon ground ginger

1 teaspoon cinnamon

1/2 teaspoon nutmeg

1–2 teaspoons sea salt or to taste

4 sprigs fresh rosemary

Prep Time:
30 minutes

Cook Time:
5–8 hours

Serves:
5

1. In a large skillet, heat the coconut oil over medium to medium-high heat.

2. Sprinkle the shanks on all sides with salt and pepper and sear them in the hot oil about 3–4 minutes per side or until all browned.

3. Place the lamb shanks in a slow cooker and set aside. In the same skillet you seared the shanks in, add the sliced onions and cook until the onions start to brown.

4. Add the garlic and sauté just until fragrant.

5. Add the strained tomatoes, peach preserves, ginger, cinnamon, nutmeg, and sea salt and whisk together, bringing to a simmer.

6. Pour the sauce over the lamb shanks, place the rosemary sprigs on top, and cook on high for 5 hours or on low for 8 hours.

Something Extra: *There's nothing more family-style than beautifully slow cooked lamb shanks in a blanket of savory and subtly sweet sauce. This recipe tastes terrific and is worth making simply because it smells great while cooking. I like to serve it with a big green salad topped with my Everyday Paleo Vinaigrette (p. 78).*

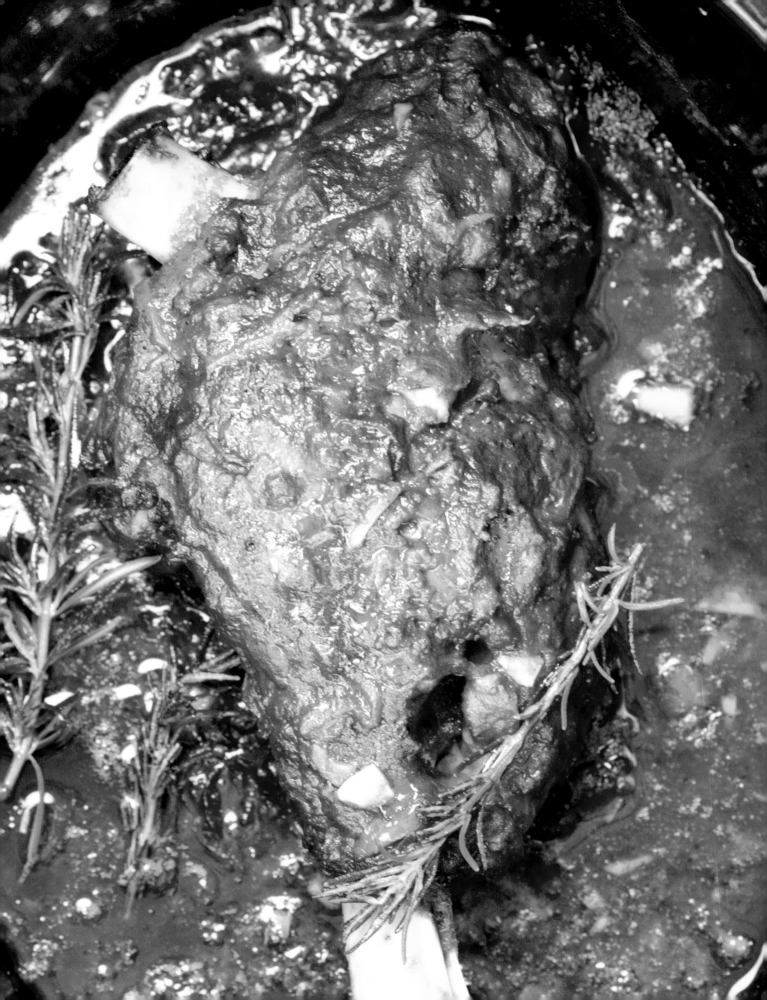

Soups and Stews

Homemade Chicken Broth

Leftover chicken carcass from Whole Greek Chicken (p. 122) or 2 pounds leftover cooked chicken parts (bones, skin, etc.)

1 yellow onion, diced

4 celery stalks, diced

5–6 garlic cloves

2 teaspoons each sea salt and black pepper

Prep Time:
30 minutes

Cook Time:
4 hours

Serves:
6

1. Place the chicken carcass or chicken parts in the bottom of a large stockpot.

2. Add enough cold water to cover the chicken parts and then add the diced vegetables, garlic cloves, and the salt and pepper.

3. Bring the water to a boil and then turn heat to low so that it's just at a simmer.

4. Simmer uncovered for 4 hours.

5. Strain the chicken broth, let it cool, then store the liquid gold in a covered glass jar in the refrigerator.

6. Discard the cooked veggies and leftover chicken parts (all the good stuff is now in the broth!!)

*Note – to make beef bone broth, simply follow the same directions except use left over beef bones! Do not toss those rib bones from the family style short ribs or ask for beef soup bones from your local butcher. Add all of the broth ingredients along with the beef bones into your slow cooker and cook overnight, strain the broth, cool, and store like you would the chicken broth. Easy, nutritious, and delicious!

Something Extra: *I love making my own chicken and beef bone broth, and you will find several recipes in this book that call for broth as an ingredient. Make a double or triple batch if you like, and freeze what you won't use within a week. It's easy to add frozen broth to any of your recipes. My family is rarely sick (thank you, Paleo!), but if someone is feeling a little under the weather, homemade broth is often the magic cure. Otherwise, it's simply a great way to warm up on a cold winter night. Here's a fun tip: See if you can find some chicken feet! They make an amazing chicken broth, rich in glucosamine chondroitin, collagen, and trace minerals. For some kids, using chicken feet is a crazy science experiment, but if it freaks them out, do not invite them into the kitchen for this particular recipe. (What they don't know won't hurt them!) A good source for making chicken broth with chicken feet and other bone broths can be found at NourishedKitchen.com. Don't skimp on this, the real deal is so much better than what you can buy in the store!*

Scrumptious Seafood Chowder

2 tablespoons coconut oil

1 medium white onion, diced

8 bacon strips, chopped (optional)

6 celery stalks, diced

5 cups peeled and cubed sweet potatoes

1 (13.5-ounce) can full-fat coconut milk (Native Forest brand)

2 cups Homemade Chicken Broth (p. 94)

⅔ cup clam juice

Sea salt and black pepper to taste

1 (10-ounce) can of wild caught clams, without juice

1 bay leaf

1 pound wild-caught shrimp, deveined with shells and tail removed

Handful of minced fresh parsley for garnish

Prep Time:
35 minutes

Cook Time:
45 minutes

Serves:
4–5

1. In a large soup pot, sauté the onion in coconut oil over medium heat for 4–5 minutes.

2. Add the diced bacon and cook until the bacon is crisp, stirring often.

3. Add the celery and sweet potatoes and sauté for another 4–5 minutes.

4. Add the coconut milk, chicken broth, clam juice, and black pepper and bring to a simmer.

5. Add the bay leaf and let the soup simmer for 20–30 minutes or until the potatoes are soft.

6. Using a potato masher, gently mash the cooked sweet potatoes to help thicken the chowder, making sure to still leave some of the potatoes chunky.

7. Add the shrimp to the chowder and cook for 5 minutes or until the shrimp are pink and tender.

8. While the shrimp are cooking, drain the clams and chop them into small pieces; add them to the chowder, and stir just until they are warm. Serve the soup immediately, topped with the fresh minced parsley if desired.

Something Extra: *My kids love to help make and eat this chowder, and their favorite part is helping me mash the sweet potatoes. Word of caution, however: Make sure you supervise your children if they want to help you mash the potatoes in the hot soup pot. Have them work very slowly, and guide their hands so that they don't get too close to the heat. My kids also help me throw in the diced veggies and add all of the other ingredients. Making chowder together is a great way to unwind together at the end of a long day.*

Tomato Soup with Chicken

1 small yellow onion, finely diced

2 garlic cloves, minced

5 cups diced tomatoes (fresh is best, just peel them first!)

1 (13.5-ounce) can full-fat coconut milk (Native Forest brand)

1 teaspoon sea salt, or to taste

1 teaspoon black pepper

2 tablespoons coconut oil

2–3 cups diced cooked chicken or more if desired (use leftover Whole Greek Chicken, p. 122)

Minced Italian flat leaf parsley for garnish

Prep Time:
30 minutes

Cook Time:
15–20 minutes

Serves:
4–5

1. In a large soup pot, cook the diced onions in the coconut oil over medium to medium-high heat until the onions start to caramelize.

2. Add the garlic and cook for another 1–2 minutes.

3. Add the diced tomatoes and cook for 7–10 minutes, stirring often.

4. Add the coconut milk, salt, and pepper, and heat to simmering.

5. Pour the soup mixture into a blender or food processor and blend until smooth.

6. Pour the soup back into the pot. Top with chopped cooked chicken and minced fresh parsley and serve immediately.

Something Extra: *This soup is comforting and rich, unlike most tomato soups, which can be watery and boring. Adding chicken makes it a protein packed meal, and we often eat it paired with the Asparagus and Browned Sage "Butter" (p. 192). If your kids want to help, have them press the buttons on the food processor, add the seasoning to the soup pot, and top their own bowls of soup with pieces of chicken.*

Hungarian Stew

2 tablespoons coconut oil or ghee

2 pounds beef stew meat

2 carrots, cut into ½-inch rounds

1 green bell pepper, diced

1 small white onion, diced

6 garlic cloves, minced

4 tablespoons smoked paprika (yes, it seems like a lot, but trust me, this amount is typical for Hungarian Stew)

2 teaspoons caraway seeds

5 ounces tomato paste (Bionaturae brand)

6 cups beef broth (p. 94)

2 cups peeled and diced winter squash or sweet potatoes

Sea salt and black pepper to taste

Prep Time:
45 minutes

Cook Time:
2–2 ½ hours

Serves:
6

1. In a large soup pot, heat the coconut oil or ghee over medium heat.

2. Add the stew meat and brown for 5–7 minutes.

3. Add all of the veggies to the browned beef along with the garlic, stir well, and cook for 10 minutes.

4. Add the paprika and caraway seeds and mix well.

5. Cook for another 5 minutes.

6. Pour in the tomato paste and beef broth, mix well, and bring to a boil.

7. Turn the heat down so that the stew is just at a simmer and cook uncovered for 1 hour.

8. Add the diced winter squash or sweet potatoes and cook for another 1 to 1½ hours.

9. Before serving, season with sea salt and black pepper to taste.

Something Extra: *This traditional Hungarian Stew is great on a cold winter night with the family. Make this recipe instead of turning to electronics and grumpiness, as many families do when the sun goes down earlier. Throw down an old blanket in the living room, and enjoy a winter night stew picnic! After dinner, get the family moving by playing a game of charades or Simon says, enjoying one another's company as only a family can.*

Fiesta Chicken Soup

2 tablespoons coconut oil

½ medium yellow onion, diced

1 red bell pepper, diced

1 Anaheim pepper, diced

2 garlic cloves, minced

1 tablespoon ground cumin

⅛ teaspoon chipotle powder

1 teaspoon poultry seasoning

2 cups diced fresh tomatoes

4 cups Homemade Chicken Broth (p. 94)

2 tablespoons tomato paste (Bionaturae brand)

3 cups shredded cooked chicken (e.g., leftovers from Whole Greek Chicken, p. 122)

Sea salt and black pepper

Cilantro leaves, diced avocado, and lime wedges as garnish

Prep Time:
40 minutes

Cook Time:
20 minutes

Serves:
4–5

1. In a large soup pot, heat the coconut oil over medium heat and add the diced onions and peppers.

2. Sauté until the veggies start to soften, approximately 5–7 minutes.

3. Add the garlic, cumin, chipotle powder, and poultry seasoning and mix well until all the veggies are coated with the seasoning.

4. Add the diced tomatoes, chicken broth, and tomato paste and mix well.

5. Add the diced chicken and bring to a simmer for 10 minutes.

6. Season with salt and pepper to taste and serve topped with cilantro leaves, diced avocado, and lime wedges.

Something Extra: *This soup is out-of-this-world easy and delicious. Have your family make this meal together and experiment with the toppings. For instance, I suggest adding a sprinkle of dried oregano, shredded green cabbage, diced bell peppers, sliced radishes, and if you're adventurous, a few dashes of hot sauce.*

Everyday Paleo Chili Verde

2 ½ pounds pork shoulder roast

2 tablespoons coconut oil

1 yellow onion, diced

4 garlic cloves, minced

1 tablespoon ground cumin

½ teaspoon smoked paprika

½ teaspoon black pepper

2 cups Homemade Chicken Broth (p. 94)

2 pounds tomatillos

1 jalapeño

1 bunch cilantro

Juice from 1 lime

Sea salt

Prep Time:
40–50 minutes

Cook Time:
3 hours

Serves:
5–6

1. Cut the pork roast into ½-inch cubes.

2. In a large soup pot, heat the coconut oil over medium-high heat and add the pork once the oil is hot enough to sizzle when you add a chunk of meat.

3. Brown the pork pieces for 4–5 minutes, then remove them with a slotted spoon and set aside.

4. Add the onions and garlic to the hot oil and pork drippings and sauté for 7–10 minutes or until the onions start to brown.

5. Turn the heat down a bit and add the cumin, paprika, and black pepper to the onions and garlic and mix well (the mixture will be kind of pasty).

6. Add the chicken broth and mix well, making sure to scrape all the goodness off the bottom of the pan.

7. Return the pork to the liquid in the soup pot and bring to a boil.

8. Turn heat down to low and let the pork simmer.

9. While the meat simmers, peel and wash the tomatillos. Dry them well and in a large skillet over medium heat char them along with the jalapeño, turning often, until the skins start to blacken (about 10 minutes).

10. Place the charred tomatillos, jalapeño, cilantro, and lime juice into a food processer or blender and blend until smooth.

11. Add the processed tomatillo mixture to the simmering pork, season the chili verde with a little sea salt, and simmer on low for 2–2½ hours, stirring occasionally, or until the pork is fall-apart tender. The sauce will reduce and become thicker over the course of cooking.

12. Taste and add more salt if needed. Serve with sliced avocado or guacamole and cilantro for garnish.

Something Extra: *This dish is definitely one of our favorite family meals. I like to make it on the weekends when we can let it sit and simmer during the afternoon. The house fills with delicious smells, and I know that little Rowan will soon be at the counter helping me to mash "ab-o-cados" (as he calls them) for guacamole. I often make a double batch of this recipe and freeze half for busy weeks ahead. You can also make it in a slow cooker. Simply follow all of the steps above, and once you have reached the final stage, transfer all of the contents to a slow cooker for 6–8 hours on low or for 4–5 hours on high (instead of cooking it on the stove for 2–2½ hours).*

Everyday Paleo Chili Colorado

7 dried New Mexico chilies

3 dried California chilies

3 dried chilies de arbol (I recommend El Guapo brand for all the suggested dried chilies; they are found at most major grocery stores, or online at Amazon)

4 cups water

1 yellow onion

5 garlic cloves

2 tablespoons coconut oil

2½ pounds beef stew meat

2 tablespoons ground cumin

2 tablespoons dried oregano

2 cups beef broth (p. 94)

12 ounces tomato paste (Bionaturae brand)

Sea salt and pepper

Diced avocado or guacamole and cilantro leaves for garnish

Prep Time:
50–60 minutes

Cook Time:
2½ hours

Serves:
5–6

1. Rinse the dried chilies and place them in a pot with the 4 cups water.

2. Bring to a boil, turn the heat off, and let the chilies soak in the water for 30 minutes.

3. While the chilies are soaking, dice the onion and mince the garlic cloves.

4. Heat the coconut oil in a large soup pot and add the onions; cook them on medium heat until they start to brown.

5. Add the garlic and beef to the onions and brown the beef for 7–10 minutes.

6. Add the cumin, oregano, beef broth, tomato paste, salt, and pepper to the beef.

7. Bring to a boil, turn heat down to medium-low or low, and let the beef simmer. While the beef is simmering, it's time to prepare the chilies. Do not throw out the liquid that the chilies have been soaking in; it will be needed!

8. Remove the stems from each chili; then place the chilies into a food processor along with half of the liquid that the chilies were boiling in. Process the chilies until smooth.

9. Strain the ground chilies through a sieve into the pot with the beef. Use a spoon to help the contents through the sieve, leaving behind the seeds and any bits of pepper skin.

10. Pour the remaining chili-cooking-liquid through the sieve and into the pot as well.

11. Bring to a boil, turn back down to low, and let the Chili Colorado simmer for 2 hours or until your meat is tender. Serve with diced avocado and cilantro leaves.

Something Extra: *Like my Chili Verde, this recipe can also be made in your slow cooker if desired. Simply follow all of the above directions, and instead of cooking on the stovetop for 2 hours, transfer it to a slow cooker for 6–8 hours on low or 4–5 hours on high. Have your kids help you with the dried chilies. They can rinse the chilies, add them to the pan, and cover them with water. It's fun to see the chilies rehydrate, and to turn them into a paste in the food processor. Just be sure everyone washes their hands well with warm soapy water after handling the chilies. They are mellow in flavor, but your eyes will sting if you accidently rub them before washing your hands.*

Meaty Meals

Brined and Sauced Baby Back Ribs

2 racks baby back ribs

Brine

1 cup Chardonnay (optional)
1 sprig fresh rosemary
½ cup apple cider vinegar
8 cups water
½ tablespoon sea salt

Dry rub

1 tablespoon garlic powder
½ tablespoon sea salt
½ tablespoon black pepper
Korean BBQ Sauce (p. 76) or Brother Mark BBQ Sauce (p. 74)

Prep Time:
20 minutes plus
overnight for brining

Cook Time:
1½ hours

Serves:
4

1. In a large stockpot or a small ice chest, mix together the brine ingredients.

2. Place the ribs in the brine, making sure the racks are completely covered, and put the container in the refrigerator overnight.

3. The next day, when you are ready to grill, heat your barbeque over low heat.

4. Remove the ribs from the brine and generously cover them with the dry rub.

5. Cook on the top rack of your barbeque on low for 1 hour, turning occasionally.

6. Generously slather both sides of the racks with BBQ sauce and cook for another 30 minutes. Brush on more BBQ sauce before serving.

Something Extra: *The first time we made these ribs, they didn't even make it to the table. We all stood around and devoured them as they were removed from the grill. I wish I had a video of my boys with BBQ sauce covering their faces and the rare bonus of a few minutes of quiet. Brining is key to the preparation of these ribs, by the way, so do not skip that step.*

Everyday Paleo Stuffing

4 tablespoons coconut oil

1 medium yellow onion, diced

1 pound mild Italian pork or beef sausage, casing removed and crumbled (US Wellness Meats)

4½ cups diced mushrooms

6 celery stalks, diced

4 carrots, diced

¼ cup Homemade Chicken Broth (p. 94)

1 tablespoon diced fresh sage

½ teaspoon minced fresh thyme

½ cup finely chopped unsweetened dried cherries

½ cup slivered almonds

4 garlic cloves, minced

Sea salt and black pepper to taste

Prep Time:
30 minutes

Cook Time:
1 hour

Serves:
5

1. Preheat the oven to 350°F.

2. In a large soup pot heat the coconut oil over medium heat, then sauté the onions until translucent.

3. Add the sausage and brown.

4. Add the mushrooms, celery, carrots, chicken broth, sage, thyme, cherries, almonds, garlic, salt, and pepper.

5. Mix well, bring to a simmer, and cook for 5–10 minutes or until the vegetables begin to absorb the chicken broth.

6. Transfer to a 9 × 13-inch glass baking dish, cover tightly with aluminum foil, and bake for 30 minutes.

7. Uncover and bake for an additional 15 minutes.

Something Extra: *Stuffing was never my favorite part of holiday dinners, but now I love it! This stuffing is so good that I have been known to make it throughout the year as a meal on its own. Try pairing this recipe with the Whole Greek Chicken with Roasted Garlic (p. 122). Let your kids help you add all of the ingredients to the pot and stir. Teach your little ones about fresh herbs—which one is sage, which one is thyme, and how to take the thyme leaves off the twigs. This recipe is all about starting new and healthier traditions with your loved ones!*

Pear and Ground Pork-Stuffed Winter Squash

3 acorn squash, cut in half and seeds removed

Coconut oil, sea salt, nutmeg

½ medium yellow onion, diced

2 tablespoons coconut oil

1 pound ground pork

2 carrots, diced

Sea salt and black pepper

2 tablespoons minced Italian parsley

2 tablespoons minced fresh sage

1 tablespoon minced fresh thyme leaves

2 garlic cloves, minced

2 Bosc pears, peeled, cored, and diced

¼ cup chopped almonds

Prep Time:
40 minutes

Cook Time:
1½ hours

Serves:
3–4

1. Preheat the oven to 350°F.

2. Dot the inside of each acorn squash with coconut oil and sprinkle each with a little sea salt and nutmeg.

3. Place the acorn squash cut side up in a large glass baking dish and add 1 cup of water to the bottom of the dish; cover tightly with aluminum foil.

4. Cook the squash in the oven for 45 minutes or until fork-tender.

5. Meanwhile, in a large skillet, sauté the onions in the coconut oil until they start to turn brown.

6. Add the ground pork, carrots, and a little sea salt and pepper (about ½ teaspoon each) and cook until the pork is no longer pink.

7. Add the parsley, sage, and thyme and cook for another 4–5 minutes.

8. Add the garlic, pears, and almonds and stir just until warm.

9. Taste the stuffing and add more salt or seasoning if desired.

10. Stuff each acorn squash with big a spoonful of the pork mixture, return to the hot oven, and bake for an additional 10 minutes.

Something Extra: *This is an extremely versatile dish that can be made with ground beef or lamb rather than ground pork. We have also stuffed the mixture into little sugar pumpkins for a bit of variety. I would also suggest that you double or triple this recipe to feed a crowd. This is a very festive dish so you can also serve it during the holidays! Fresh herbs are imperative to make the flavors pop, so don't skimp with the dry stuff. This dish deserves the real thing! Let your kids help you dot the insides of the squash with the coconut oil and sprinkle in the nutmeg before baking!*

Ground Pork and Apple Sliders

2 pounds ground pork

½ cup minced white onion

1½ cups finely diced apple

1½ tablespoons Italian seasoning

1 teaspoon garlic powder

1½ teaspoons sea salt

1 teaspoon black pepper

Prep Time:
15 minutes

Cook Time:
20 minutes

Serves:
5

1. Mix the ground pork with the minced onions, diced apples, and spices. If you prefer a milder slider, first sauté the minced onions in a little coconut oil.

2. Evenly separate the meat mixture into 8–10 portions and form those into patties.

3. Cook on a grill or in a large skillet over medium heat for 7–10 minutes per side or until the patties are done all the way through and no longer pink in the middle. You can serve them like burgers wrapped in lettuce with some Homemade Ketchup (p. 70) or topped with sauerkraut. (I recommend Bubbies brand sauerkraut unless you want to make your own; directions for homemade kraut are at EverydayPaleo.com.) We also enjoy the sliders topped with a fried egg and a few dashes of hot sauce.

Something Extra: *Sliders and burgers are so easy to make, especially when time is an issue, but burgers can get boring. Variety is important for families, and the added bite of the onions and sweetness of the apples make these sliders special. My kids love these more than any other burger I make. Another great advantage of this recipe is that it works for breakfast, lunch, or dinner, and if you make a double batch, you can have plenty on hand for leftovers during the week when you need something to grab quickly or pack into lunches.*

Best Ever Chicken Wings

2½ pounds chicken wings

Marinade

2 garlic cloves, minced

1 teaspoon grated fresh ginger

3 tablespoons coconut aminos or Bragg Liquid Aminos

1 tablespoon sesame oil

½ cup apple juice

Sesame seeds and minced chives or green onions for garnish

Prep Time:
20 minutes plus 30 minutes at least for marinating

Cook Time:
35–40 minutes

1. Preheat your oven to 425°F.

2. In a large bowl, whisk together the marinade ingredients.

3. Add the chicken wings to the bowl of marinade and mix well until all the wings are coated. Let the wings marinate in the fridge for at least 30 minutes, but 1–2 hours make the wings tastier.

4. Line a baking sheet with aluminum foil and place 1 wing at a time on the baking sheet, making sure to shake off any excess marinade. Do not crowd the wings on the sheet.

5. Roast the wings for 35–40 minutes, turning them over halfway through the cooking time. Serve sprinkled with the sesame seeds and chives.

Something Extra: *These wings are beyond good, and they're great party food! The first time I made them, little Rowan sat on top of the kitchen table and demolished nearly every single wing in sight. It takes a lot for Rowan to not make a peep for more than five minutes, but these wings did the trick. Make sure you make plenty, because I promise they will be a hit. My kids like to help me whisk the marinade and sprinkle on the sesame seeds and green onions, but the only requirement for this meal is that you have fun! The recipe pairs well with the Kale Chips (p. 170) or Riced Cauliflower (p. 176).*

Chicken Cacciatore

2 tablespoons coconut oil

1 yellow onion, diced

3 celery stalks, diced

3 carrots, diced

3 garlic cloves, minced

¼ cup balsamic vinegar

3 cups strained tomatoes (Bionaturae brand) or tomato sauce

1 cup Homemade Chicken Broth (p. 94)

¼ cup full-fat canned coconut milk (Native Forest brand)

1 tablespoon dried parsley

1 tablespoon dried thyme

3 cups sliced white mushrooms

Sea salt and black pepper

4–6 boneless, skinless chicken breasts

Prep Time:
40 minutes

Cook Time:
45 minutes–1 hour

1. Preheat your oven to 375°F.

2. In a large soup pot, heat the oil over medium-high heat.

3. Add the onion, celery, and carrots and sauté until the onions start to brown.

4. Add the garlic and sauté just until fragrant.

5. Turn the heat up to high and pour in the balsamic vinegar; then turn the heat down to medium or medium-high and reduce the vinegar by half, stirring often so that it doesn't burn.

6. Add the strained tomatoes or tomato sauce, chicken broth, and coconut milk to the pot and stir.

7. Add the parsley, thyme, and mushrooms and bring to a boil.

8. Turn the heat down to low, season with salt and pepper to taste, and let the sauce simmer while you prep the chicken.

9. Place the chicken breasts in a large casserole dish and sprinkle each side with a little salt and pepper.

10. Pour the sauce from the soup pot over the chicken, cover tightly with foil, and bake in the preheated oven for 45 minutes to 1 hour or until the chicken is no longer pink in the middle.

Something Extra: *This is total comfort food and one of John's favorite meals. I love the richness of the sauce; it really livens up the chicken. We often serve this dish with the Zucchini Salad (p. 184) or Spaghetti Squash (p. 148), but it's just fine alone. The sauce can also be used with meatballs or ground beef for a quick and easy weeknight meal.*

Whole Greek Chicken with Roasted Garlic

4½- to 5-pound whole chicken

1 lemon, cut in half

Sea salt

Dried parsley

Pepper

2–4 bulbs garlic

Prep Time:
25 minutes

Cook Time:
1½ hours

Serves:
4

1. Preheat the oven to 400°F.

2. Remove the giblets from the chicken and save them to add to Homemade Chicken Broth if you like.

3. Rinse the chicken and dry it well with paper towels.

4. Stuff the cavity of the chicken with the halved lemon.

5. Generously sprinkle the entire chicken with plenty of sea salt, dried parsley, and pepper.

6. Place the chicken breast side up in a roasting pan and truss it with cooking twine (tie the ends of the legs together).

7. Cut the tops off the garlic bulbs to expose the cloves and set aside.

8. Roast the bird uncovered in the preheated oven for 30 minutes, add the garlic bulbs to the roasting pan next to the chicken, and cook for another 45 minutes to an hour or until the chicken is brown and crispy and reaches an internal temperature of 190°F. Eat with the roasted garlic spread on pieces of the chicken.

Something Extra: *It doesn't get easier or more delicious than this meal, which is sure to please the entire family. My boys love the crispy legs and wings, and there is nothing quite like roasted garlic spread on tender chicken. This recipe is great served with the Kale and Parsnip Sauté (p. 204), and it also goes well with Roasted Squash Bites (p. 194) or even a simple Chopped Salad (p. 198). Be sure to save the carcass of the chicken to make Homemade Chicken Broth (p. 94). For big families, you might want to make two of these roasted chickens!*

One Pot Chicken Drumsticks

2 tablespoons coconut oil

8 chicken drumsticks

Sea salt and black pepper

1 tablespoon poultry seasoning

1 medium yellow onion, cut into large chunks

4 garlic cloves, minced

1 cup diced fresh tomatoes

3–5 small zucchini, cut into large chunks

Prep Time:
25 minutes

Cook Time:
30 minutes

Serves:
3–4

1. In a large skillet, heat the coconut oil over medium-high heat until hot enough to sizzle when you add the drumsticks. Generously season the drumsticks with salt and pepper, add to the hot oil, and sear for 5–7 minutes or until browned on all sides.

2. Sprinkle the poultry seasoning on top of the drumsticks and add the onions, garlic, and tomatoes.

3. Cover, turn the heat down to medium or medium-low, and simmer for 15 minutes.

4. Add the zucchini and cook for an additional 5 minutes or until the chicken is no longer pink in the middle.

Something Extra: *This is an extremely simple weeknight meal that tastes as though you put in a lot of effort. We love it with the Chopped Broccoli Salad (p. 178). Here's a quick tip for a fast meal: Before you start to cook the chicken, throw some sweet potatoes wrapped in foil in a 400°F oven to serve alongside the chicken; they will be done by the time the rest of the meal is complete!*

Curry Chicken Salad

3 cups shredded cooked chicken

1 small apple, cored and diced

1½ cups diced celery

3 green onions, diced

1¼ cup Mayonnaise (p. 62)

1 tablespoon curry powder (or more to taste)

¼ cup slivered almonds

Sea salt and black pepper to taste

Prep Time:
25 minutes

Serves:
5–6

In a large bowl, mix all the ingredients. Serve the salad on its own, on top of cucumber slices, or scooped onto endive or lettuce leaves.

Something Extra: *Jaden loves this salad in his lunch, and I like to make a big curry chicken salad on the weekends so that I can quickly pack a container of it, along with cucumber slices or carrot sticks, before we run out the door. My favorite apples to use in this salad are Fujis because they stay nice and crisp and add a nice crunch. To change the taste of this easy meal, you can substitute dried dill or rosemary for the curry powder. If you decide to use dill instead of the curry, leave out the apples and add diced dill pickles instead. You could also add chopped hard-boiled eggs for more versatility. Remember—be creative, and let your little ones decide what they want to try next!*

Chinese Chicken Salad

3 cups shredded cooked chicken

1 (12-ounce) bag kelp noodles (Sea Tangle brand)

2 cups diced red cabbage

1 cup diced fresh mandarin oranges

4 green onions, diced

¼ cup sesame oil

2 tablespoons coconut aminos or Bragg Liquid Aminos

1 teaspoon grated fresh ginger

Black pepper

3 tablespoons sesame seeds

Prep Time:
25 minutes

Serves:
5–6

Mix all the salad ingredients together and enjoy!

Something Extra: *Although I'm not a huge fan of "Paleo-ish" substitutes for Neolithic foods, these kelp noodles are fun and do not have any scary additives or other non-Paleo ingredients. They do not, however, have a lot of flavor on their own, so I add coconut aminos and ginger to give them a yummy zing. Then, the kids have fun slurping them up.*

Shrimp in Horseradish Mustard Sauce

2 tablespoons coconut oil

4 tablespoons Mayonnaise (p. 62)

I pound large wild-caught raw shrimp, shelled, deveined, and tails removed

4 teaspoons prepared horseradish

2 tablespoon lemon juice

4 green onions, diced

2 tablespoons Dijon mustard

Black pepper to taste

Minced Italian parsley for garnish (optional)

Prep Time:
25 minutes

Cook Time:
3–5 minutes

Serves:
3–4

1. In a large skillet, heat the coconut oil over medium heat.

2. Add the shrimp and sauté just until pink, about 3 minutes, and remove from the heat.

3. In a small bowl, mix together the remaining ingredients.

4. When the shrimp are done, toss them with the sauce or simply pour the sauce over them and serve immediately, topped with a little fresh minced parsley if desired.

Something Extra: *Recipe credit for this deliciously simple meal goes to the lovely Sheryl Seib, wife of my business partner at Everyday Paleo Lifestyle and Fitness, Jason Seib. I love easy-to-prepare recipes, and this one certainly fits the bill. The flavor combinations are truly scrumptious—the creaminess of the mayonnaise cuts the bite of the horseradish, and even my little Rowan loves the tangy, creamy, yummy "shrimpies!" Try it for a fast lunch or dinner, and you can even substitute your favorite white fish in place of the shrimp.*

Coconut Shrimp Cocktail

4–6 cups water

½ a lemon, sliced into thin rounds

Sea salt to taste

1 pound extra-large, wild-caught raw shrimp, shelled and deveined

1 cup full-fat canned coconut milk (Native Forest brand)

¼ cup minced red onion

2 garlic cloves, minced

¼ cup diced fresh cilantro

Juice from ½ lemon

¼ cup finely diced red bell pepper

Pinch cayenne pepper

Hot sauce (optional)

Diced mango (optional)

Prep Time:
30 minutes

Cook Time:
4 minutes

Serves:
2–3

1. Pour the water into a large saucepan and throw in the lemon slices and a big pinch of sea salt.

2. Bring the water to a boil over high heat.

3. Add the shrimp to the boiling water, turn the heat down to medium or medium-low, and cook the shrimp for 3 minutes or until they turn pink.

4. Once the shrimp are done, remove immediately from the hot water and cool in ice water to stop the cooking process.

5. Once the shrimp are cool, pour into a strainer and set aside to drain.

6. While the shrimp are draining, stir together the remaining ingredients. Add the shrimp to the coconut milk mixture and toss to coat.

7. Chill the shrimp cocktail in the refrigerator for at least 30 minutes before serving. Serve with a few dashes of hot sauce like Tapatio or even Sriracha if desired and garnish with a few more cilantro leaves or diced mango (optional).

Something Extra: *This creamy shrimp cocktail is a cool summertime treat. For variety, add diced cucumbers (seeds removed), or if you like the dish spicier, add a minced fresh jalapeño pepper (seeds removed). I like to serve this recipe as an appetizer when entertaining guests, but our family enjoys it as a meal or a snack.*

Seared Ahi or Salmon

¼ cup sesame seeds

1 teaspoon black pepper

½ teaspoon sea salt

1 (½ pound) sushi-grade wild-caught Ahi filet

1 (½ pound) sushi-grade wild-caught salmon filet

1–2 tablespoons coconut oil

Sriracha Mayo (p. 72) or coconut aminos for dipping

Prep Time:
15 minutes

Cook Time:
6 minutes

Serves:
2–3

1. Mix the sesame seeds, black pepper, and sea salt and spread the mixture evenly on a large plate.

2. Take the fish filets and gently press them on both sides and edges into the sesame seed mixture so that the filets are totally covered with the seeds.

3. In a large skillet, heat the coconut oil over medium-high heat. Before you put the fish in the pan, make sure the oil is nice and hot!

4. Place the filets in the pan and cook for 2–3 minutes on each side, so that the outside edges just start to cook but the fish is still raw in the middle.

5. Thinly slice the sesame crusted seared filets and serve with Sriracha Mayo or coconut aminos and wasabi for dipping.

Something Extra: *Can you say "date night" food? My kids also love sushi, but when I find a good sushi-grade filet, I often selfishly wait until the kids are in bed so that I can pour a glass of wine and share this meal with John, just the two of us. Slowing down and reconnecting are key to the Paleo way of living, and this is a simple and delicious way to share.*

Tuna Patties

3 (5-ounce) cans tuna packed in water, drained

2 eggs

½ tablespoon dried dill

½ teaspoon sea salt

¼ teaspoon black pepper

2 tablespoons coconut oil

Prep Time:
20 minutes

Cook Time:
10 minutes

Serves:
3–4

1. Mix the tuna with the eggs, dill, salt, and pepper.

2. In a large skillet, heat the coconut oil over medium to medium-high heat. Make sure the oil is nice and hot!

3. Form the tuna mixture into 11–12 small, slightly flattened patties and cook in the hot oil for 2–3 minutes per side.

4. You will not be able to fit all 11–12 in your pan at the same time, so you might have to add more oil for each batch. Make sure the patties are brown before you flip them so that they hold together! Serve with my Simply Coleslaw (p. 202) and topped with Garlic Lemon Aioli (p. 72).

Something Extra: *This is one of our go-to lunch recipes. It's fast, inexpensive, protein packed, and tasty. I always like to have Mayonnaise on hand for making sauces, and the Garlic Lemon Aioli (page 72) on top of these tuna patties gives them exceptional flavor. Substitute canned salmon if you prefer, and the addition of Simply Coleslaw (page 202) makes an especially yummy meal. My kids love to help me make the tuna into patties, and although the end result isn't always beautiful, it's all about having fun together as a family!*

Fish Tacos with Spicy Slaw

1–2 pounds wild-caught cod filets

Marinade

Freshly squeezed juice from 1 lime

1 tablespoon olive oil

¼ teaspoon chipotle powder (Penzy's brand)

1 teaspoon ground cumin

½ teaspoon sea salt

Spicy Slaw (p. 206)

Butter or Romaine lettuce leaves

Diced fresh cilantro

Sliced radishes

Lime wedges

Prep Time:
35 minutes

Cook Time:
10 minutes

Serves:
3–4

1. In a medium-sized bowl, whisk together the marinade ingredients.

2. Put the fish filets in the bowl of marinade and gently rub the marinade into them; let the fish soak for at least 15 minutes.

3. In the meantime, prepare the Spicy Slaw (p. 206).

4. Rinse and dry several large butter or Romaine lettuce leaves, dice up a bunch of cilantro, slice a few radishes, and slice up some lime wedges. Set these garnishes aside.

5. Now, time to cook the fish! Heat a large skillet over medium heat and add the fish and all the remaining marinade to the hot pan.

6. Cook the filets on each side for about 3–4 minutes or until the fish flakes easily, but do not overcook!

7. Remove the skillet from the heat and use your spatula to gently flake apart the filets. Serve the fish flakes in a lettuce leaf topped with Spicy Slaw, diced cilantro, sliced radishes, and a squeeze of lime.

Something Extra: *Honestly, I could eat these fish tacos every single day! I also like to make them with shrimp. The subtle spiciness of the coleslaw on top of the flaky, fresh fish and the crunch of the radishes and jicama are divine. (My mouth is watering as I write this. I may have to take a break and make some fish tacos right now!) I recommend doubling this recipe if you are making it for more than two or three people.*

Savory Salmon and Cool Peach Salsa

Wild-caught salmon filets (as many as you need to feed your family)

Sea salt and black pepper

2 tablespoons coconut oil (or more depending on how many filets you make)

Cool Peach Salsa

2 cups diced peeled peaches (or diced mango)

1 cup halved grape or cherry tomatoes

½ cup minced red onion

1 cup chopped cilantro leaves

1 jalapeño, seeds removed and minced (optional)

2–3 garlic cloves, minced

1 teaspoon ground cumin

Pinch cayenne pepper

Juice from 1 lime

1 tablespoon olive oil

Sea salt and black pepper to taste

Prep Time:
40 minutes

Cook Time:
12–15 minutes

Serves:
5–6

1. Preheat your oven to 350°F.

2. In a large bowl, gently mix all the peach salsa ingredients and place in the fridge to keep cool.

3. Meanwhile, sprinkle both sides of the salmon filets with sea salt and black pepper and heat the coconut oil over medium-high heat in a large ovenproof skillet.

4. Once the oil is nice and hot, place the salmon filets in the skillet. Fry the filets for 1–2 minutes per side, or until the fish has a nice golden sear on both sides.

5. Place the pan with the salmon into the preheated oven and cook for another 5–10 minutes, depending on the thickness of the salmon. Be sure to check often for doneness to avoid drying out your fish. If you can easily dig into the middle of the filet with a fork and the center of the filet looks translucent, pull the salmon out of the oven—it's done! The salmon will continue cooking even after being pulled from the heat, so make sure you take it out before it's cooked all the way through to ensure a moist piece of fish.

6. Once the salmon is done, serve topped with a big scoop of the peach salsa.

Something Extra: *Kids like fruit, and succulently seared salmon likes to be topped with fruit. It's a match made in heaven! When I make this peach salsa with Rowan, my challenge is to get the diced peaches in the bowl with the other ingredients before Rowan eats all of them. This meal is a delightful summertime treat, and feel free to serve the peach salsa over grilled chicken or steaks, as well as other seafood options.*

Smoked Salmon and Poached Egg Salad

Organic arugula or organic mixed salad greens

Wild-caught smoked salmon (Aldrin & Son's Wild Caught Alaskan Salmon)

Poached eggs

Lemon and Garlic Aioli (p. 72)

Prep Time:
15 minutes

Cook Time:
3–4 minutes per egg

Serves:
As many as you like

There are no specific amounts for this dish; make as much or as little as you would like, depending on how many folks you are feeding. What we do:

1. Put a big handful of arugula or salad mix on a plate.

2. Break apart the smoked salmon and top the greens with as much of it as you like.

3. On top of the salmon and greens place one or two poached eggs, and then pour on top of the salad as much or as little of the Lemon Garlic Aioli as you like.

4. Season with black pepper.

5. Eat and enjoy! I even recommend this salad for breakfast.

How to make the perfect poached egg:
Now you may ask, how on earth does one poach an egg successfully? Well, I'll walk you through it step by step, and then you'll be an egg-poaching expert!

6. First, fill a small saucepan ¾ of the way full with water and bring to a boil.

7. While you are waiting for the water to boil, gently crack an egg into a small bowl.

8. Once the water is boiling, hold the bowl with the egg over the pan close to the water and gently slip the cracked egg into its hot bath.

9. Turn the heat down to just a simmer and do not disturb the egg until you see that the whites are cooked, 3–4 minutes.

10. Gently remove the poached egg from the water with a shallow slotted spoon. Once you get the hang of it, you can poach two eggs at a time!

Something Extra: *I can't tell you how much I love poached eggs, and my family shares my affection for this recipe with the yummy, runny yolks over peppery greens with flaked, smoked salmon and lemony homemade aioli. You can make this salad with canned, wild-caught salmon, too, or even a salmon filet that has been sprinkled with some sea salt and black pepper and then quickly seared in little bit of coconut oil in a hot pan. Wild-caught fish is an important addition to this natural way of eating, as it provides a wonderful food source of important Omega-3s, as well as all-important protein.*

Sloppy Joes

2 tablespoons coconut oil

⅓ cup finely chopped yellow onion

2 carrots, finely chopped

2 pounds ground beef

3 garlic cloves, minced

1½ tablespoons chili powder

1 tablespoon Italian seasoning

6 ounces tomato paste (Bionaturae brand)

1½ cups Brother Mark BBQ Sauce (p. 74)

Sea salt and black pepper to taste

Portobello mushrooms or large lettuce leaves of your choice

Prep Time:
20 minutes or longer if you have to make the BBQ sauce

Cook Time:
30–40 minutes

Serves:
5

1. Heat the coconut oil in a large skillet over medium heat and sauté the onions and carrots until the onions begin to brown.

2. Add the ground beef and cook until the meat just starts to brown.

3. Add the garlic and dried spices and mix well.

4. Add the tomato paste and the BBQ sauce and cook for another 5–7 minutes. Meanwhile, remove the stems from the portobello mushrooms and then using a spoon remove the ribs gently from the underside of the portobello mushrooms.

5. In a large skillet, heat another tablespoon of coconut oil over medium heat and cook the mushrooms on each side for 5–6 minutes or until they are tender. Serve the Sloppy Joes on the mushrooms like a sandwich, or wrapped in lettuce leaves.

Something Extra: *Remember when this meal came in a can? Not anymore, and this is so much better than the "real thing." The name is no joke; you really are required to get messy! Quick family tip: Not all kids like mushrooms, so if that option doesn't fly with your family, use lettuce leaves, scoop the meat with Sweet Potato Chips (p. 172), or just eat the meat with a spoon. I suggest serving these Sloppy Joes with my Poblano Roasted Sweet Potatoes (p. 182) and Simply Coleslaw (p. 202). Make sure to have plenty of napkins ready!*

Curry Burgers

2 pounds ground beef

2 tablespoons curry powder

3 garlic cloves, minced

¼ cup minced yellow onion

1 teaspoon sea salt

1 teaspoon black pepper

8–10 large butter or Romaine lettuce leaves

1 small cucumber, thinly sliced into rounds

1 small apple, thinly sliced

Curry Spread (p. 68)

Prep Time:
30 minutes

Cook Time:
10–12 minutes

Serves:
5

1. Mix together the beef, curry powder, garlic, onion, salt, and pepper.

2. Split the meat evenly into 10 portions and shape those portions into burgers.

3. Grill or pan-fry over medium to medium-high heat for 5–7 minutes on each side (adjust time depending on thickness of the burgers, but if the meat is evenly split into 10, this cooking time should result in a medium-well burger).

4. Place the burgers on large lettuce leaves and top with the thinly sliced cucumbers, apples, and some of the Curry Mayo.

Something Extra: *You don't have to resort to the standard fare on burger night. By adding some spice, you can kick dinner up a notch. I always ask people to be creative in the kitchen, so you can experiment with your own flavor combinations. Think Italian burgers by trading Italian seasoning for curry powder, or make a Mexican food inspired burger by using chili powder. My kids love to help me form the beef into patties, and once the burgers are done, they like adding the apple and cucumber slices. Enjoy these tasty burgers with Carrot French Fries (p. 196).*

Spaghetti Squash and Meatballs

1 large spaghetti squash, cut in half and seeds removed

Sauce

2 tablespoons coconut oil

1½ cups diced white onion

2–3 garlic cloves, minced

3 cups strained tomatoes (Bionaturae brand) or tomato sauce

3 heaping tablespoons tomato paste (Bionaturae brand)

1½ tablespoons Italian seasoning

1 tablespoon dried basil

1 teaspoon black pepper

1 teaspoon sea salt

Meatballs

1 pound ground beef

1 pound ground pork

1 teaspoon sea salt

½ teaspoon black pepper

½ tablespoon dried basil

½ tablespoon dried oregano

2–3 garlic cloves, minced

Prep Time:
45 minutes

Cook Time:
45–50 minutes

Serves:
5–6

1. Preheat the oven to 450°F.

2. In a large baking dish, place the squash cut side down and add 2 inches of water. Cover tightly with aluminum foil and bake for 35–40 minutes or until the insides of the squash can easily be removed with a fork.

3. Meanwhile, while your squash is baking, start your sauce. In a large stockpot, heat the coconut oil over medium heat and sauté the onions until translucent.

4. Add the garlic and sauté for another minute or two or just until the garlic is fragrant.

5. Add the strained tomatoes (or tomato sauce) and tomato paste and mix well.

6. Add the remaining spices, bring the sauce to a simmer, and turn heat down to low. While the sauce is simmering, make your meatballs.

7. Use your hands to mix the spices into the ground beef and pork.

8. Form the meat mixture into small golf ball-size meatballs and drop these gently into the simmering tomato sauce.

9. Once all the meatballs are in the sauce, cook for 10 minutes or until the meatballs are no longer pink in the middle.

10. Scrape the insides of the cooked spaghetti squash out with a fork and serve topped with the meatballs and sauce.

Something Extra: *Little hands like to make meatballs, and meal prep is much more fun when everyone makes this family-style dinner together. Spaghetti squash really is nature's pasta. Serve it with Zucchini Salad (p. 184) or a simple green salad with Balsamic Vinaigrette (p. 78).*

Mini Meatloaves

1 pound ground beef

1 pound ground pork

1½ teaspoons sea salt

½ teaspoon black pepper

2 garlic cloves, minced

1 teaspoon onion powder

1 teaspoon dried parsley

1 cup finely diced carrots

1 cup finely diced spinach leaves

Coconut oil or ghee

Homemade Ketchup (p. 70)

Prep Time:
30–40 minutes

Cook Time:
15–20 minutes

Serves:
5

1. Preheat your oven to 350°F.

2. In a large mixing bowl, mix together the meat, all the seasonings, and the diced veggies.

3. Grease a muffin tin with coconut oil or ghee.

4. Measure out ⅓ cup meat mixture into each muffin space.

5. Spread a generous amount of Homemade Ketchup on the top of each mini meatloaf and bake for 15–20 minutes or until the meatloaves are no longer pink in the middle.

Something Extra: *Meatloaf is a Fragoso family favorite, and these mini meatloaves are great when I do not have time to bake my usual giant meatloaf, which takes over an hour in the oven plus prep time. My kids love the fact that we make our own ketchup, and our homemade sauce is awesome on these Mini Meatloaves. Serve this with Kale and Pomegranate Salad (p. 190) or Roasted Squash Bites (p. 194).*

Mexican Beef Skewers
With Chipotle Cream and Cilantro Pesto

2 pounds sirloin steak cut into 2-inch cubes

Organic cherry tomatoes

Small bamboo skewers

Marinade

6 garlic cloves

½ cup olive oil

2 tablespoons lemon juice

¼ cup unsweetened organic cocoa powder (Rapunzel Organic Cocoa Powder)

2 tablespoons ground cumin

2 teaspoons cinnamon

½ teaspoon chipotle powder

1½ teaspoons sea salt

Chipotle Cream (p. 68) and Cilantro Pesto (p. 68) for dipping

Prep Time:
50–60 minutes, plus at least 30 minutes of marinating time

Cook Time:
15 minutes

Serves:
4–5

1. Put all the marinade ingredients in a food processor and process until smooth.

2. The marinade will be a thick paste; use a rubber spatula to scrape it into a medium-sized mixing bowl.

3. Place the beef cubes into the marinade and stir well, making sure that all the pieces are well coated.

4. Cover the bowl and let the beef marinate in the refrigerator for at least 30 minutes, but overnight is best if possible.

5. Meanwhile, prepare the Chipotle Cream (p. 68) and Cilantro Pesto (p. 68).

6. Using small skewers, assemble the skewers by alternating a beef cube and a cherry tomato until all of your skewers are filled.

7. Heat your BBQ over medium-high heat and grill the skewers on each side for 3–4 minutes for medium to medium rare.

8. Serve the skewered beef with Chipotle Cream and Cilantro Pesto for dipping.

Something Extra: *The smell of the marinated beef on the grill is tantalizing! Have everyone help assemble the skewers, and feel free to use other veggies, such as zucchini, onions, and bell peppers, as well as the recommended cherry tomatoes. You can also make just veggie skewers to go along with the steak skewers, and dip them in the Chipotle Cream and Cilantro Pesto. I like to make Poblano Roasted Sweet Potatoes (p. 182) to accompany this dish.*

Vietnamese Lamb Lettuce Wraps

2 pounds ground lamb

2 tablespoons coconut oil

½ cup minced yellow onion

3–4 garlic cloves, minced

½ cup minced cilantro stems

¼ cup lime juice

3 tablespoons fish sauce, (Red Boat Fish Sauce)

2 teaspoons Sriracha sauce

Several bok choy leaves, stems removed

1 large cucumber, peeled and diced

1 bunch cilantro leaves, diced

1 red or yellow bell pepper, diced

Prep Time:
40 minutes

Cook Time:
15 minutes

Serves:
4–5

1. Brown the ground lamb in a large skillet over medium heat.

2. Once the lamb is cooked, remove the meat from the skillet with a slotted spoon, place it in a bowl, and set aside, leaving behind any grease from the cooked lamb.

3. In the same skillet, and the coconut oil and melt over medium heat.

4. Add the onions and sauté until they start to brown, add the garlic and cilantro stems, and cook for another 3–4 minutes.

5. Return the lamb to the skillet with the onions, garlic, and cilantro stems.

6. Whisk together the lime juice, fish sauce, and Sriracha and pour over the lamb (adjust the amount of Sriracha depending on your desired spice level, or omit if you do not like anything spicy). Stir the sauce and lamb mixture together just until warm and remove from heat.

7. To serve, fill a bok choy leaf with the lamb mixture and top with the diced cucumbers, cilantro, bell pepper, and more Sriracha if desired. Pick it all up like a taco, and eat!

Something Extra: *My family enjoys an eclectic variety of foods, and this meal is a simple way to introduce new flavors to your family. You can substitute ground pork, beef, or veal, but the flavors of this dish especially complement lamb. You can also exchange butter lettuce leaves or large red or green leaf lettuce for the bok choy. Each family member can build his or her own wrap with the toppings of choice. I also recommend trying these wraps topped with the Spicy Sriracho Mayo (p. 72).*

Another quick tip – Bok choy leaves can also make an excellent bun replacement for burgers. They hold up better than lettuce; we use one leaf on top of the burger and another on the bottom.

Egg Dishes

Pesto Baked Eggs

Baking ramekins—one for each egg

Eggs—as many as you need to feed your family

Coconut oil or ghee

Pesto

1 cup walnut halves and pieces (soaked overnight in water and drained)

6 garlic cloves

1 cup extra-virgin olive oil

1 teaspoon sea salt

3½ cups fresh basil

Juice from ½ a lemon

Prep Time:
40 minutes

Cook Time:
20–25 minutes

Serves:
Makes a little over 2 cups of pesto

1. Preheat your oven to 350°F.

2. Put the walnuts, garlic, olive oil, and sea salt in a food processor. Process until smooth.

3. Add the basil and lemon juice to the walnut mixture and process again until smooth.

4. Grease your baking ramekins with coconut oil or ghee. Crack one egg into each ramekin.

5. Using a spoon or, if you want to get fancy, a squirt bottle, drizzle on top of each raw egg at least 1 tablespoon of the pesto.

6. Place the ramekins on a baking sheet and bake for 20–25 minutes or until the eggs are set and the whites do not jiggle when you shake the ramekins.

7. With a butter knife, gently loosen the eggs from the sides of the ramekins and quickly flip over onto a plate to remove. Top with more pesto if desired and enjoy!

Something Extra: *This is a simple way to make baked eggs, but whatever you do, don't confine the pesto to this recipe. We love this pesto spread on chicken, seafood, and veggies. We also enjoy it mixed with spaghetti squash or added to frittatas. As far as the baked eggs are concerned, my kids like to add grated sweet potatoes, diced ham, diced spinach, or sun-dried tomatoes to their eggs before baking. There are a million options to liven up the same old egg, so get creative, let your kids choose what to add to the mix, and enjoy!*

Winter Squash Hash and Eggs

2 tablespoons coconut oil

1 small red onion, thinly sliced

1½ cups diced crimini mushrooms

2 cups peeled and diced winter squash (I recommend butternut squash or delicata squash, but any winter squash will do)

½ cup finely diced ham or prosciutto

1 teaspoon dried rubbed sage

Sea salt and black pepper to taste

6 eggs

Finely chopped parsley for garnish

1. In a large skillet, sauté the thinly sliced onion in the coconut oil over medium heat until translucent.

2. Add the diced mushrooms and squash and cook for another 7–10 minutes or until the squash is tender all the way through.

3. Add the ham, sage, salt, and pepper and stir together.

4. Spread the cooked hash evenly over the bottom of the skillet and make 6 small holes in the hash.

5. Break an egg into each of the holes in the hash, cover with a lid, and cook over medium-low to low heat until the whites of the eggs are done all the way through but the yolks are still runny.

6. Scoop out an egg with plenty of the surrounding hash and serve in bowls or on small plates. Garnish the hash with minced parsley if desired.

Prep Time:
40 minutes

Cook Time:
15–20 minutes

Serves:
3–4

Something Extra: *One of the first kitchen lessons I received from my mom was how to crack an egg, so for fun let your little helpers crack their own eggs! This meal is not just for breakfast, so try having it for dinner when you have a bit more time to have fun in the kitchen with your little ones. You can also substitute sweet potatoes for the winter squash and cooked bacon for the ham or prosciutto. Summertime hash ideas include grated zucchini and chopped spinach. Keep experimenting!*

Creamy Breakfast Quiche

1 pound thick cut bacon, diced

1 large bunch baby spinach

12 eggs

1 cup diced mushrooms

3 green onions, chopped

3 tablespoons full-fat canned coconut milk (Native Forest brand)

2 cloves garlic, minced

1 teaspoon onion powder

1 tablespoon Italian seasoning

Black pepper to taste

Prep Time:
35 minutes

Cook Time:
55 minutes

Serves:
5–6

1. Preheat your oven to 375°F.

2. Brown the diced bacon in a large skillet.

3. Meanwhile, rinse the spinach in a strainer and let it drip dry while you finish cooking the bacon.

4. Spread the cooked bacon evenly over the bottom of a 9x13-inch glass baking dish.

5. Take the spinach and squeeze out any water left in it. Spread the spinach on top of the bacon.

6. In a large bowl whisk the eggs. Add the last 7 ingredients to the eggs and stir together.

7. Pour the entire mixture over the spinach and bacon. To make sure all the spinach is completely covered by the egg mixture, use your hand and press on top of the spinach until the egg mixture sits on top of the spinach layer evenly.

8. Cover the quiche tightly with foil and bake in the preheated oven for 30 minutes. Remove the foil and bake for another 20–25 minutes or until the eggs are cooked through in the center. You'll know the quiche is done when you jiggle the pan and the center does not move.

Something Extra: *Credit for this recipe goes to Sheryl Seib, whom I admire greatly. Our family loves this amazing dish, and I am excited to share it with all of you.*

Family Frittata

2 tablespoons coconut oil

1 cup grated sweet potato

1 cup grated zucchini (after the zucchini has been grated, place it in a clean kitchen towel and squeeze out any excess moisture)

2 tablespoons minced Italian parsley

1 cup diced ham

12 eggs, whisked

Prep Time:
30 minutes

Cook Time:
30 minutes

Serves:
5–6

1. Preheat the oven to 350°F.

2. In a large ovenproof skillet, heat the coconut oil over medium to medium-high heat, add the grated sweet potato, and cook until the sweet potatoes are soft and start to brown.

3. Add the diced ham and cook another 3–4 minutes.

4. Add the zucchini and sauté just until the shreds start to soften. Add the parsley and mix well.

5. Spread the veggie and ham mixture evenly over the bottom of the skillet and pour the whisked eggs evenly over the top of the veggie-ham mixture.

6. Cook on medium-low heat for 3–4 minutes or until you see that the edges of the frittata are starting to cook.

7. Put the entire pan into the preheated oven and cook for another 10–15 minutes or until the frittata is firm in the middle when you shake the pan.

8. Slice the frittata as you would a pizza and serve it up.

Something Extra: *Frittatas are one of our favorite ways to start the day, and I like the fact that we often have leftovers that are perfect for lunch. I can't stress enough the importance of creativity when making Paleo meals. Yes, this book is filled with recipes, but you have the freedom to make each one your own by simply switching the veggie or protein ingredients to whatever you have on hand. In this case, try adding chopped broccoli or spinach rather than zucchini, or leave out the sweet potato and add diced bell pepper and onions. Have your kids decide what they want in the Family Frittata that day, and let them help you prepare the meal.*

Tuna Stuffed Eggs

6 hard-boiled eggs

2 tablespoons Mayonnaise (p. 62)

1 green onion, diced

2 teaspoons lemon juice

2 teaspoons Dijon or yellow mustard

Sea salt and black pepper to taste

1 (6-ounce) can tuna, drained

Chopped dill pickles (optional)

Prep Time:
30 minutes

Serves:
6

1. Peel the hard-boiled eggs and slice them in half lengthwise.

2. Take the yolks out of each half and put them in a small bowl.

3. Add the mayo, diced green onion, lemon juice, mustard, salt, and pepper to the yolks.

4. Mash the yolks with all of the added ingredients and mix well.

5. Stir the tuna into the yolk mixture.

6. Spoon this mixture into the hollowed-out egg halves and enjoy!

Something Extra: *My family loves this deviation from standard deviled eggs, and they're great for a picnic or potluck dish. For variation, you can substitute canned wild-caught salmon for the tuna. Make a double batch to have on hand for after-school snacks or a quick lunch, and let your kids help you mix the filling and stuff the eggs. Rowan and Jaden scoop the tuna mixture into the eggs and eat them before they even hit their plates! These also get a big thumbs-up from my sixteen-year-old, Coby, who says they "rock!"*

Egg Salad

12 hard-boiled eggs, diced

1 cup diced celery

1 cup diced dill pickles (Bubbies brand)

1 tablespoon minced fresh dill

1/3 cup Mayonnaise (p. 62)

Sea salt and black pepper to taste

4 bacon strips, cooked and crumbled (optional)

Prep Time:
20 minutes

Serves:
5

Mix all the ingredients and serve with bell pepper strips, cucumber slices, or in lettuce wraps!

Something Extra: *I love scooping up this salad with bell pepper strips or even celery sticks, and having a bowl of it in the fridge ready to go makes a great lunch or after-school snack. Get your kids in the kitchen with this one by letting them peel the hard-boiled eggs.*

Sides, Salads and Small Plates

Kale Chips Two Ways

Sesame chips

1 bunch kale

1 tablespoon olive oil

1 tablespoon sesame oil

1 tablespoon coconut aminos or Bragg Liquid Aminos

Prep Time:
30 minutes

Cook Time:
12 minutes

Serves:
5

1. Preheat your oven to 300°F.

2. Wash and dry the kale. Make sure the kale does not have any excess moisture to ensure a crispy, crunchy chip.

3. Tear the kale into bite-sized pieces, discarding the tough spines of the leaves.

4. In a small bowl, whisk together the olive oil, sesame oil, and coconut aminos or Bragg Liquid Aminos.

5. In a large bowl, add the torn kale leaves and pour the oil and aminos mixture over the leaves. Use your hands to rub the oil and aminos mixture into the kale leaves until they are all well coated.

6. Spread the kale leaves evenly on foil-lined baking sheets; make sure the leaves are not crowded or overlapping.

7. Sprinkle all the kale pieces with sesame seeds.

8. Bake approximately 12 minutes, but watch carefully to make sure the chips do not burn. Once they are crispy they are done.

Garlic chips

1 bunch kale, torn into bite-sized pieces

2 tablespoons olive oil

2–3 garlic cloves, minced

Sea salt

1. Preheat your oven to 300°F.

2. Mix together the olive oil and minced garlic.

3. Follow the same directions for preparing the kale for the garlic chips as you do for the sesame chips. Pour the oil and garlic onto the torn kale, and use your hands to toss the kale and rub the oil and garlic into the leaves.

4. Arrange evenly on foil-lined baking sheets and bake for approximately 12 minutes, watching carefully that the chips do not burn.

5. Sprinkle with a little sea salt and eat!

Something Extra: *We discovered kale chips a few years ago, and we have never looked back. Kale chips satisfy that desire for a crunchy snack, but instead of being grain-based or trans fat-laden and highly processed, they are nutrient-packed and tastier than any chemically flavored chip I've ever had. Mixing up the flavors is fun; my kids love the sesame chips the best out of the two, but my vote goes to the garlic chips. Whenever anyone asks me how to get kids to eat greens, my first answer is Kale Chips!*

Sweet Potato Chips

1 large sweet potato

¼ cup coconut oil (to start, but you may need to add more)

Sea salt

Prep Time:
20 minutes

Cook Time:
6 minutes

1. Peel the sweet potato and cut into thin round slices using either a mandoline slicer or the slicing blade on a food processor.

2. In a large skillet add the coconut oil and heat over medium-high until the oil is hot enough to sizzle when you put in a slice of sweet potato.

3. Fry the sweet potato chips just a few at a time, making sure not to crowd the pan.

4. Once the edges of the sweet potato slices start to curl and turn golden brown, flip them with metal tongs and cook for another minute or two, but watch them carefully so they do not burn.

5. When the chips are done, remove them from the pan and put them on a plate with paper towels to drain. Sprinkle with sea salt and enjoy!

Something Extra: *These chips are a bit time-consuming but well worth the effort. We all love these treats, and they go well with the Curry Burgers (p. 146), the Baby Back Ribs (p. 110), and the Best Ever Chicken Wings (p. 118). We also like to make them on the weekend for lunch with the Curry Chicken Salad (p. 126).*

Turkey "Sushi" Rolls

Turkey rolls

Sliced turkey deli meat (Applegate Farms brand)

Cucumbers, in thin matchstick pieces

Carrots, in thin matchstick pieces

Avocado, thinly sliced

Sesame seeds (optional)

Dipping sauce

¼ cup Mayonnaise (p. 62)

½ teaspoon coconut aminos or Bragg Liquid Aminos

1 tablespoon chopped chives

Prep Time:
15 minutes

Serves:
As many as you like

1. Lay a piece of turkey deli meat flat on a cutting board.

2. Layer the matchstick cucumbers and carrots, plus the avocado slices, down the length of the turkey slice.

3. Tightly roll the turkey slice around the veggies.

4. Roll the entire turkey roll in a plate of sesame seeds if desired.

5. Slice into small rolls.

6. Mix all the sauce ingredients and serve with the turkey rolls for dipping.

Something Extra: *I have found that the Applegate Farms brand of lunchmeat holds together best out of all the brands I've tried, and I also trust their ingredients. This is a great lunch box idea, as well as a fun after-school snack. My boys like helping me make the recipe, and we often substitute thinly sliced jicama and bell peppers for the cucumber, carrot, and avocado.*

Riced Cauliflower

1 head cauliflower

3 tablespoons coconut oil

3 green onions, diced

2 garlic cloves, minced

1 egg, whisked

1 teaspoon coconut aminos or Bragg Liquid Aminos

1 tablespoon sesame oil

Black pepper

Prep Time:
30 minutes

Cook Time:
15 minutes

Serves:
5

1. Rinse and dry the cauliflower and cut into florets.

2. Place the florets into a food processor and process until they are finely minced, looking like rice!

3. In a large skillet, melt the coconut oil over medium heat.

4. Add the cauliflower and sauté for 5–6 minutes.

5. Add the green onions and garlic and sauté with the cauliflower for another 2–3 minutes.

6. Push the cauliflower mixture to the side of the pan and pour in the whisked egg onto the empty side of the pan and cook until the egg begins to firm.

7. Mix the egg into the cauliflower mixture and add the coconut aminos or Bragg Liquid Aminos, the sesame oil, and black pepper.

8. Taste your riced cauliflower and add more aminos or sesame oil if desired.

Something Extra: *This Riced Cauliflower is faster and tastier than rice itself. It pairs well with several recipes in this book— Best Ever Chicken Wings (p. 118), One-Pot Chicken Drumsticks (p. 124), Pork Green Curry (p. 84), and Slow Chicken Curry (p. 88). See if you can fool your friends with this one; I promise you it will become one of your favorite side dishes for almost any meal. We also like to add chopped broccoli, bell peppers, or thinly sliced cabbage. To make it a one-dish meal, add some cooked ground pork, diced ham, or diced chicken.*

Chopped Broccoli Salad

3 cups finely chopped broccoli florets

1 small apple, cored and diced

9 strips of bacon, cooked and crumbled (US Wellness Meats, Niman Ranch, or Applegate Farms)

3 green onions, diced

¼ cup Balsamic Vinaigrette (p. 78)

Prep Time:
30 minutes

Serves:
5

Place all the ingredients except the vinaigrette into a large bowl, drizzle with the Balsamic Vinaigrette, toss, and enjoy! Taste and add more dressing if desired.

Something Extra: *Chopped Broccoli Salad is as easy as it is delicious, and it's a great way to get some variety into the typical steamed or roasted broccoli routine. I like it served with grilled steak, but it also pairs nicely with the Family-Style Short Ribs (p. 86) or with leftover chicken cut into pieces and placed on top. Then, you turn a salad into a meal! My kids are not huge fans of broccoli, but they really like this salad because the pieces are small and easy to chew. Besides, who doesn't like a salad with bacon?*

Roasted Beet Salad

4 cups peeled and cubed beets

¼ cup coconut oil, melted

5 cups baby arugula

2 celery stalks, diced

¼ cup very thinly sliced red onion

⅓ cup chopped walnuts

¼ cup Everyday Paleo Vinaigrette (p. 78)

Prep Time:
30 minutes

Cook Time:
30 minutes

Serves:
4–5

1. Preheat your oven to 450°F.

2. Evenly spread the cubed beets on a baking sheet, drizzle with the melted coconut oil, and sprinkle with sea salt.

3. Roast the beets for 25–30 minutes or until they're tender all the way through.

4. In a large bowl, toss together the arugula, celery, and red onions.

5. On another baking sheet spread the chopped walnuts and bake in the already hot oven for 4–5 minutes; watch carefully and do not burn the walnuts.

6. Add the beets, walnuts, and vinaigrette to the salad, toss, and serve!

Something Extra: *This salad is tasty, tangy, and sweet from the beets. My kids like roasted beets all by themselves, so I sometimes roast extra beets for them to munch on and use what's left to make this salad. Serve this recipe with the Whole Greek Chicken with Roasted Garlic (p. 122) or any protein of your choice.*

Poblano Roasted Sweet Potatoes

¼ cup coconut oil

½ teaspoon sea salt

1 teaspoon ground cumin

1 teaspoon cinnamon

½ teaspoon black pepper

5 cups peeled and diced sweet potatoes

1 poblano pepper, seeds removed and diced

4–5 garlic cloves, minced

Prep Time:
20 minutes

Cook Time:
30 minutes

Serves:
5

1. Preheat your oven to 400°F.

2. Melt the coconut oil and in a small bowl whisk the spices and the oil together.

3. In a large mixing bowl add the diced sweet potatoes, minced poblano pepper, and minced garlic.

4. Pour the oil and spice mixture over the potatoes and stir well until all the sweet potatoes are coated.

5. Pour the sweet potatoes into a large glass baking dish and roast for 25–30 minutes or until the potatoes start to brown and are soft all the way through, stirring halfway through the cooking time.

Something Extra: *I have so many memories of how my kids talked when they were very little. Rowan is now four and just starting to grow out of some of his cute expressions and mispronunciations. I'm a little sad to say goodbye to this stage. Since Rowan could talk, he has always loved his "Seat Tatoes." Have your kids help you put the diced sweet potatoes into the bowl, and stir in the oil and spices. They can also help you measure the spices and set the timer on the stove. Kids can do just about everything that you do in the kitchen as long as you supervise them and teach them early what's hot or sharp and, therefore, unsafe to touch. Give your children the confidence and freedom that they long for by letting them help, and you'll be amazed at what they're capable of doing even at a very young age. Serve these sweet potatoes with the Mexican Beef Skewers (p. 152).*

Zucchini Salad

2 small zucchini, sliced with spiral vegetable slicer or a julienne slicer

1½ tablespoons minced Italian parsley

2 tablespoons minced sun-dried tomatoes packed in olive oil

⅓ cup roughly chopped kalamata olives

¼ cup red onions thinly sliced with a mandoline

1 tablespoon extra-virgin olive oil

½ tablespoon lemon juice

Sea salt and black pepper

Prep Time:
30 minutes

Serves:
3—4

1. Place the zucchini, parsley, sun-dried tomatoes, olives, and onions in a small mixing bowl.

2. This is a raw salad, no need to cook the sliced zucchini!

3. Drizzle on the olive oil and lemon juice and sprinkle with a little sea salt and black pepper.

4. Toss the salad; then let it sit in the fridge for 15—20 minutes before serving.

Something Extra: *Plain green salad can get boring for some folks, so having options in the salad department is never a bad thing. John was surprised that this simple salad was so flavorful. Now, the entire family requests it often. Having special staples on hand like olives and sun-dried tomatoes can really jazz up an ordinary side dish, so keep your food interesting by adding surprising flavors to otherwise unsurprising foods.*

No Potato Salad

I head of cauliflower

6 eggs, hard-boiled and diced

½ a small red onion, finely diced

3-4 celery stalks, finely diced

I cup diced dill pickles

¾ cup Mayonnaise (p. 62)

I tablespoon dried dill

I teaspoon yellow mustard

Black pepper to taste

Prep Time:
40 minutes

Serves:
5–6 minutes

1. Cut the cauliflower into large florets and steam for about 7-8 minutes or until tender but NOT mushy.

2. While the cauliflower is steaming add the diced egg, onion, celery, and pickles to a large mixing bowl and set aside.

3. Once the cauliflower is steamed, remove the cauliflower from the pan and let it cool in the fridge for 5-10 minutes.

4. Remove the cauliflower from the fridge and chop it into small pieces. Add the cauliflower to the bowl with the diced egg, onion, celery, and pickles.

5. Add the remaining ingredients and mix well.

Something Extra: *When I was growing up, every time there was a family gathering, we could always expect my mom to make her amazing potato salad! My favorite thing about my mom's potato salad was having that first bite right after she finished making it, when the potatoes were still just a little bit warm. This is my mom's recipe, except instead of the standard white potato, I substituted with steamed cauliflower! I have made this several times for people who both do and do not eat Paleo and everyone has loved this salad. They are often fooled that this isn't the "real deal!"*

Gingered Rainbow Chard

2 tablespoons coconut oil

4 bunches rainbow chard, tough
stems removed and leaves cut
into small ribbons

3 garlic cloves, minced

2 teaspoons grated fresh ginger

⅓ cup Homemade Chicken Broth
(p. 94)

¼ teaspoon red chili flakes
(optional)

Sea salt and black pepper to
taste

Sesame seeds for garnish

Prep Time:
30 minutes

Cook Time:
15 minutes

Serves:
4–5

1. Heat the coconut oil in a large skillet or wok over medium heat.

2. Add the ribbons of rainbow chard and the garlic and sauté until the chard starts to wilt.

3. Add the ginger, chicken broth, chili flakes, and salt and pepper and mix well until warmed through, about another 2–3 minutes.

4. Serve sprinkled with sesame seeds if desired.

Something Extra: *I like chard because of its interesting flavor, which some describe as bitter, but in a good way. The stuff is also beautiful to look at. Ginger mellows the taste of the greens, and the garlic gives it a kick. I suggest serving it with the Baby Back Ribs (p. 110).*

Kale and Pomegranate Salad

*1 bunch kale, ribs removed and
leaves cut into thin ribbons*

*2 tablespoons walnut oil or extra-
virgin olive oil*

1 tablespoon lemon juice

¼ cup pomegranate seeds

½ cup chopped walnuts

Sea salt and black pepper

Prep Time:
30 minutes

Serves:
4–5

1. Put the kale in a medium mixing bowl. In a small bowl, whisk together the oil and lemon juice.

2. Pour this mixture over the kale and, using your hands, rub the oil and lemon juice into the kale.

3. Add the pomegranate seeds, walnuts, and a sprinkle of sea salt and black pepper and toss with the kale. Taste the salad and add more salt and pepper or lemon juice if needed. You can also use raisins or currants in place of the pomegranate seeds.

Something Extra: *Raw kale, you say? Yes, indeed. Rubbing the oil and lemon into the thinly sliced ribbons of kale is the key to making this salad yummy. Pomegranate seeds add color and pop, and kids love them. So, have fun scooping them out of the fruit and tossing them in the salad. Pair this recipe with the Hungarian Stew (p. 100), Sloppy Joes (p. 144), or any other protein you choose. The salad is also delightful at any holiday because of its festive colors!*

Asparagus and Browned Sage "Butter"

2 tablespoons ghee or coconut oil

1½ tablespoons minced fresh
sage

2 cups diced asparagus

Sea salt and black pepper

Prep Time:
15 minutes

Cook Time:
8 minutes

Serves:
3–4

1. In a medium skillet, melt the ghee or coconut oil over medium heat.

2. Add the minced sage and sauté until the sage starts to brown and crisp.

3. Add the asparagus to the browned sage and sauté until the asparagus is tender but still crisp, about 5 minutes.

4. Season with a little sea salt and black pepper and serve!

Something Extra: *This side dish tastes too good to be so easy to make, and the frying sage smells fantastic. The herb really adds to the flavor of the asparagus, too. Serve it with the Mini Meatloaves (p. 150), Pesto Baked Eggs (p. 158), or the Pear and Ground Pork-Stuffed Winter Squash (p. 114).*

Roasted Squash Bites

3 tablespoons coconut oil or ghee

1 tablespoon cinnamon

½ teaspoon sea salt

6 cups peeled, cubed butternut squash

Prep Time:
30 minutes

Cook Time:
45 minutes–1 hour

Serves:
5–6

1. Preheat your oven to 400°F.

2. Melt the coconut oil or ghee and in a small bowl whisk together the oil, cinnamon, and sea salt.

3. Pour the seasoned oil over the cubed squash and toss until all the pieces are coated with the oil mixture.

4. Spread the cubed squash into a large glass baking dish and bake for 45 minutes to an hour.

Something Extra: *I have made this many times for my family and also for Thanksgiving; it's scrumptious. Feel free to use other winter squash options besides butternut. Any winter squash will do, even small sugar pumpkins, but I like butternut because it's easier to peel and cut than some of the other possibilities. I use a regular vegetable peeler to peel my squash; it works much better than trying to carefully remove the skin with a paring knife. Plus, it's safer.*

Carrot French Fries

¼ *cup coconut oil*

3–4 carrots, peeled and cut into matchstick pieces

Sea salt

Prep Time:
25 minutes

Cook Time:
10 minutes

Serves:
3–4

1. In a large skillet, heat the coconut oil over medium to medium-high heat.

2. Add the carrot French fries and fry for 6–8 minutes or until the carrots start to crisp and turn brown, turning them often in the hot oil.

3. Remove the carrots from the oil with a slotted spoon, and sprinkle them with a little sea salt before serving.

4. Serve with some Paleo Ranch (p. 64) for dipping! These will not be super crispy crunchy like regular potato fries, but the coconut oil and carrots together taste so good that you'll love them, I promise.

Something Extra: *Fries are fun, so why not make carrot fries? I serve these with my Curry Burgers (p. 146), Baby Back Ribs (p. 110), and as a snack to go with the Tuna-Stuffed Eggs (p. 166). Delight your family with this new way to make fries.*

Make Your Own Chopped Salad

Dressing

4 tablespoons extra-virgin olive oil

2 tablespoons balsamic vinegar

1 teaspoon dried parsley

½ teaspoon onion powder

Sea salt and black pepper to taste

Salad

Romaine lettuce

Artichoke hearts

Tomatoes

Cucumbers

Carrots

Celery

Olives

Broccoli

Bell peppers

Mushrooms

Apples

Green onions

Sliced almonds

Prep Time:
30 minutes

Serves:
As many as you like

1. Chop all or any combination of the ingredients into small pieces and arrange in different bowls.

2. In a small jar with a lid, add all the salad dressing ingredients.

3. Let everyone build their own salad, and let the kids shake up the salad dressing before they pour it on.

Something Extra: *Often getting kids to eat healthier foods has everything to do with giving them the power to choose and have some fun in the process. This salad, though maybe a bit more time-consuming than most, is a great way to encourage your kids to try new things without even asking them. Just have the options available, and see what happens. Take turns shaking the dressing and passing around the salad ingredients, but say nothing about what anyone picks or doesn't pick. Focus instead on happy conversation and a good time.*

Zucchini Sticks

I cup almond meal (use the coarser almond meal, such as that from AmminNut.com or Trader Joe's)

I teaspoon sea salt

I tablespoon Italian seasoning

Black pepper

2 eggs

2 medium zucchini, cut into sticks

1. Preheat your oven to 350°F.

2. Grease a cookie sheet with some ghee or coconut oil and set aside. In a medium mixing bowl, stir together the almond meal, sea salt, Italian seasoning, and pepper. In another medium bowl beat the two eggs.

3. Place all the zucchini sticks into the egg wash and coat well.

4. Transfer 4 zucchini sticks at a time to the almond meal mixture and toss until the zucchini sticks are evenly coated.

5. Place the zucchini sticks on the greased cookie sheet; do not crowd them.

6. Bake for 30 minutes in the preheated oven or until the zucchini are soft and the outside starts to brown, turning them halfway through the cooking time.

Nut allergy alternative

2 eggs

½ teaspoon sea salt

2 tablespoons Italian seasoning

½ teaspoon black pepper

2 medium zucchini cut into sticks

2 tablespoons ghee or coconut oil

1. Beat the two eggs in a medium bowl, add the sea salt, Italian seasoning, and pepper, and mix well.

2. Toss all of the zucchini sticks into the egg mixture and coat well.

3. Heat the ghee or coconut oil in a large skillet over medium heat and wait for the oil to get nice and hot.

4. Place the egg-coated zucchini sticks in the hot pan.

5. Cook for 2–3 minutes per side, turning often, or until the zucchini sticks are browned.

Serve either kind of zucchini stick with Paleo Ranch (p. 64).

Prep Time:
45 minutes

Cook Time:
30 minutes for breaded and 5–7 minutes for nut-free version

Serves:
6

Something Extra: *This recipe is a wonderful hands-on experience for the entire family. We like to make zucchini sticks on the weekend when we have a little more time. I prefer the ones without the almond-meal breading; they are easier to whip up and do not take as long to cook. But make both kinds, and discover what you and your family like best.*

Simply Coleslaw

2 cups finely shredded green cabbage

½ cup grated carrot

½ cup finely diced apple

¼ cup Mayonnaise (p. 62)

Sea salt and black pepper to taste

Prep Time:
20 minutes

Serves:
4

In a large mixing bowl, toss all of the salad ingredients together. Enjoy!

Something Extra: *I suggest serving this coleslaw with the Tuna Patties (p. 136) or Family-Style Short Ribs (p. 86). It is also great with the Mini Meatloaves (p. 150) or a good ol' grilled burger! This is one of my go-to side dishes when I'm in a hurry, and I sometimes add leftover diced chicken to make it a meal on its own.*

Kale and Parsnip Sauté

2–3 tablespoons coconut oil

½ yellow onion, diced

2½ cups peeled and diced parsnips

1 bunch kale, finely diced

2–3 garlic cloves, minced

1 teaspoon grated fresh ginger

Sea salt and black pepper to taste

Drizzle of olive oil

Prep Time:
30 minutes

Cook Time:
20 minutes

Serves:
5

1. Heat the coconut oil in a large skillet over medium heat. Sauté the onions in the oil until translucent.

2. Add the diced parsnips and sauté until the parsnips and onions are browned and caramelized.

3. Add the kale to the pan, cover, and cook for 2–3 minutes.

4. Add the garlic, ginger, salt, pepper, and a drizzle of olive oil. Stir well and cook for another 3–4 minutes.

Something Extra: *Parsnips are often an overlooked veggie, but we love them. Their sweetness combined with the bite of the ginger and the bitterness of the kale make a tasty accompaniment to any meal. Try this recipe with my Whole Greek Chicken with Roasted Garlic (p. 122).*

Spicy Slaw

2 cups shredded green cabbage

I cup diced mango

½ cup diced cilantro leaves

1½ cups peeled and diced jicama

I fresh jalapeño, seeds removed
and minced (optional)

¼ cup Mayonnaise (p. 62)

⅛ teaspoon chipotle powder
(Penzey's)

½ teaspoon ground cumin

Prep Time:
20 minutes

Serves:
5

Toss all of the ingredients in a large mixing bowl and enjoy!

Something Extra: *This slaw is a must for my Fish Tacos (p. 138), but don't stop there. It goes extremely well with lettuce-wrapped tacos made with ground beef seasoned with chili powder, cumin, and garlic. Also, as with some of my other salad recipes, feel free to add some diced cooked chicken or other protein to turn it into a meal. This salad includes an awesome veggie called jicama, which I suggest trying sliced into sticks and dipped into guacamole or Paleo Ranch (p. 64).*

Fruity Creations and Treats

Creamy Fruit Salad

¼ cup coconut cream

1 orange, peeled and diced

1 pear, cored and diced

1 apple, cored and diced

4 dates, pitted and chopped into small pieces

¼ cup raisins

¼ cup unsweetened shredded coconut (optional)

¼ cup chopped pecans (optional)

1 teaspoon cinnamon

Prep Time:
30 minutes

Serves:
5

1. Chill a 13.5-ounce can of full-fat coconut milk (Native Forest brand) overnight in the fridge.

2. In a large mixing bowl add all of the ingredients except for the coconut cream.

3. Open the chilled can of coconut milk and scoop out the coconut fat or cream that has separated from the water and has solidified on the top of the can.

4. Measure out ¼ cup of the coconut fat (cream) and add to the bowl and mix well.

5. Serve the salad with a few more coconut flakes and chopped pecans on top.

Something Extra: *I keep small plastic utensils for my younger kids to use when cutting fruits and vegetables. They're perfect when we make this fruit salad together. Rowan and Jaden help me cut up the fruit and scoop out the coconut cream while I chop the dates. Then, we all take turns stirring the salad. The dates lend just enough sweetness to make it taste like a dessert, and the coconut and crunchy pecans add the right amount of texture.*

Fruit Parfait

Whipped coconut cream

½ teaspoon vanilla

Mango, diced

Watermelon, diced

Blueberries

Any other diced fruit or berries of your choice

Pistachios, chopped

Prep Time:
25 minutes

Serves:
As many as you like

1. Chill a 13.5-ounce can of coconut milk in the fridge overnight (Native Forest brand).

2. Scoop out the coconut fat (cream) from the top of the can, leaving the liquid behind, but save the liquid for soups or smoothies.

3. Add the vanilla to the coconut cream.

4. Using a hand-held mixer, whip the coconut cream just as you would regular whipped cream, until fluffy!

5. Take a dessert cup and layer the diced fruit, scoop some whipped coconut cream on top, then sprinkle on some chopped pistachios. Keep on layering until the dessert cup is full.

Something Extra: *This fruit parfait is a delicious and refreshing summertime treat. Who needs ice cream when you can have fresh fruit and coconut cream? Dessert takes on an entirely different meaning when living a Paleo lifestyle. Something as simple as this turns into a special treat that everyone can feel good about eating. I like to keep a can or two of coconut milk in my fridge during the summer months just for this reason.*

Pumpkin Muffins

2 cups almond meal (AmminNut.
com)

⅓ cup coconut flour
(TropicalTraditions.com)

I teaspoon baking soda

I tablespoon pumpkin pie spice

½ teaspoon sea salt

1½ cups organic canned or
freshly cooked pumpkin

6 eggs

¼ cup raw organic honey

¼ cup melted ghee or coconut oil

I cup raisins

Prep Time:
30 minutes

Cook Time:
30–45 minutes

Makes:
16 muffins

1. Preheat your oven to 350°F.

2. In a medium mixing bowl, add the almond meal, coconut flour, baking soda, pumpkin pie spice, and sea salt, and stir well.

3. In a large mixing bowl, add the pumpkin, eggs, honey, and melted ghee or coconut oil, and mix with a hand-held beater until well blended.

4. Pour the dry ingredients into the wet ingredients and continue to blend with the hand-held mixer until smooth.

5. Fold in the raisins.

6. Grease a muffin tin with more coconut oil or ghee.

7. Use a ¼-cup measuring cup to fill each muffin space with the muffin mix and bake for 30–45 minutes or until a toothpick can be inserted into the middle of a muffin and it comes out clean. Makes 16 muffins.

Something Extra: *I do not make treats like these very often because we would eat them all the time if they were around. However, having a treat option that does not wreck our guts or leave us overly cranky or wired is always nice on special occasions. We like to make these yummy muffins now and then on the weekends, and they are awesome on Christmas morning! You can also replace the raisins with dark chocolate chips for a great party treat.*

Fried Banana Pudding

2 tablespoons coconut oil

2 bananas, sliced

¼ cup full-fat canned coconut milk (Native Forest Brand)

Raisins

Chopped nuts

Coconut flakes

Cinnamon

Prep Time:
15 minutes

Cook Time:
7 minutes

Serves:
2–3

1. Heat the coconut oil in a medium skillet over medium heat.

2. Add the sliced bananas and cook until the bananas start to bubble and mush together.

3. Add the coconut milk to the skillet with the bananas and mix together until warm and bubbly.

4. Serve the banana pudding in a dessert cup sprinkled with raisins, chopped nuts, coconut flakes, and a sprinkle of cinnamon.

Something Extra: *The first time I made this recipe it was for my oldest son, Coby. His response was: "Mmmmm, Mom, this is really good; make sure this goes in the next cookbook." Well, Coby, here you go! This banana pudding is dedicated to Coby for his honesty, passion, and love of life.*

Rocket Fuel

1 cup chopped pecans

½ cup chopped walnuts

½ cup chopped almonds

5 dates, finely chopped

2 egg whites

1 tablespoon cinnamon

Coconut oil or ghee

Prep Time:
25 minutes

Cook Time:
15 minutes

Makes:
14 cookies

1. Preheat your oven to 350°F.

2. In a large mixing bowl, add the nuts and finely chopped dates.

3. In a separate bowl, drop in the egg whites, add the cinnamon, and beat with a fork until the cinnamon is blended with the egg whites.

4. Pour the egg whites over the nuts and dates and mix until everything starts to stick together.

5. Using your hands, create balls of the nut, date, and egg white mixture (about the size of golf balls), and place onto a baking sheet greased with coconut oil or ghee.

6. Still using your hands, compact each cookie so that they hold together in the oven.

7. Bake for 15 minutes. Makes 14 cookies.

Something Extra: *I came up with these cookies when I was writing* Paleo Pals, Jimmy and the Carrot Rocket Ship. *Hence, the name "Rocket Fuel." These are a special treat and, according to Rowan, the best cookies ever! My kids enjoy helping me make them, and Jaden can now do everything on his own.*

Everyday Paleo Pumpkin Pie

Crust

½ cup hazelnuts

I cup pecans

4 tablespoons melted ghee

Pinch sea salt

Filling

I (14-ounce) can unsweetened organic pure pumpkin purée

2 teaspoons cinnamon

¼ teaspoon ground cloves

¼ teaspoon grated fresh ginger

2 eggs

½ cup raw organic honey

½ cup full-fat canned coconut milk (Native Forest Brand)

Prep Time:
40 minutes

Cook Time:
I hour

1. Preheat your oven to 350°F.

2. Place the hazelnuts and pecans in a food processor and process until the nuts are finely ground; make sure you stop before the nuts start to turn into nut butter!

3. Pour the ground nuts into a small mixing bowl, add the melted ghee and salt, and mix into a thick dough.

4. Using your hands, spread the dough evenly into a pie pan and bake for 10–15 minutes or until the crust starts to brown.

5. While the crust is in the oven, mix all of the pie filling ingredients with a hand-held mixer.

6. Once the crust is out of the oven, pour the filling into the crust, return the pie to the oven, and bake for an additional 45 minutes.

Something Extra: *I have served this pie to extended family members, friends, and even Navy Seals, all with rave reviews. Some traditions just cannot be broken, and a pumpkin pie during the holidays is one of those traditions for us. Having this recipe ensures that we can have our pie and eat it too, which is very important to me as I strive to live the healthiest life possible, both mentally and physically. I hope you enjoy it!*

EVERYDAY PALEO FAMILY COOKBOOK

Ingredient Index